The Solar System

An A–Z Guide

Franklin Watts
A Division of Grolier Publishing
New York   London   Hong Kong   Sydney
Danbury, Connecticut

Edited and designed by
Bookmark Associates, Inc.

Editors
Edward S. Barnard
Sharon Fass Yates

Author
Christina Wilsdon

Designer
Ken Chaya

Copy Editor
Kristina Bohl

Photo Researcher
Susan Ferrelli

Indexer
Aaron Murray

Consultant
Dr. Frank Summers
Astrophysicist
American Museum
of Natural History

Library of Congress Cataloging-in-Publication Data
Wilsdon, Christina.
    The solar system : an A-Z guide / by Christina
Wilsdon.
        p.   cm.
    Includes bibliographical references and index.
    Summary: A dictionary of terms, concepts, peo-
ple, and places related to the solar system, astrono-
my, and the exploration of space.
    ISBN 0-531-11710-3 (lib. bdg.)
    ISBN 0-531-16489-6 (pbk.)
    1. Astronomy Dictionaries, Juvenile. [1.
Astronomy Dictionaries.] I. Title.
QB14.W55 2000
520.3--dc21   99-342 15
                        CIP

GROLIER
PUBLISHING

A close-up, computer-colored view of Saturn's rings. (For more information about Saturn and its rings, see pages 66-67.)

The Solar System

An A–Z Guide

Table of Contents

Aldrin, Edwin

Edwin E. "Buzz" Aldrin (1930–) was the second person to set foot on the Moon. (Neil Armstrong was the first.) A U.S. Air Force pilot before becoming an astronaut, Aldrin had some new ideas that made it easier for future astronauts to work in space.

On his first space flight on *Gemini 12* in 1966, Aldrin was a pilot and a "spacewalker." A spacewalker works outside the spacecraft. On an earlier mission, astronaut Gene Cernan had become exhausted when he spacewalked. It had taken him an hour to go just 15 feet along the outside of the spaceship.

Aldrin, however, brought new equipment to help him work in weightlessness. He used a special "space wrench" that made it easier to tighten and loosen bolts. He wore special boots and carried hand tools, a rail, lines, and handholds to help him better grip the spaceship. He could brace himself against the spaceship while he worked instead of fighting to keep from floating away. Aldrin spacewalked for five and a half hours without problems.

Buzz Aldrin *posed for this photograph taken by Neil Armstrong during the Apollo 11 Moon mission.*

Three years later, Aldrin was aboard *Apollo 11*, flying to the Moon with Neil Armstrong and Michael Collins. On July 20, 1969, Aldrin and Armstrong landed the lunar module *Eagle* on the Moon. They collected rocks and set up experiments. Then they rejoined Collins in the command module and returned to Earth. SEE ALSO APOLLO PROGRAM; ARMSTRONG, NEIL; ASTRONAUTS AND COSMONAUTS.

Apollo Program

The mission of the Apollo program was to land humans on the Moon and return them to Earth. This goal was set in 1961 by President John F. Kennedy.

A three-part spacecraft was designed and built. One part was the command module, where the crew lived and worked. It would orbit the Moon but not land on it. The command module was linked to a service module, which carried most of the oxygen, water, and power. The third part was the lunar module. A Saturn rocket towering 102 meters (335 feet) high was to boost the assembly into space.

In 1967, the first Apollo flight was nearly ready. Then tragedy struck. A fire broke out in a test of the spacecraft as it sat on its launch pad on January 27, 1967, killing the three-man crew. After this disaster, several unpiloted flights were made.

Apollo 7, the first piloted mission of the Apollo program, took off on October 11, 1968, carrying its crew into Earth orbit. On December 21, 1968, *Apollo 8* took humans into space to orbit the Moon for the first time. Astronauts on *Apollo 9* practiced using the lunar module while orbiting Earth in March 1969. *Apollo 10's* crew carried out a test run for a Moon landing in May 1969, but did not descend to the Moon itself.

Then, on July 16, 1969, *Apollo 11* was launched with a three-man crew. On July 20, 1969, President Kennedy's goal became a reality. Commander Neil Armstrong and pilot Buzz Aldrin guided the lunar module, named *Eagle*, to a landing on the Moon. Meanwhile, Michael Collins remained in the orbiting command module. "The Eagle has landed," Armstrong declared after the lunar module's foot-

Armstrong, Neil

Neil Armstrong (1930–) was the first person to walk on the Moon. "That's one small step for a man—one giant leap for mankind," he said, placing his left foot on the Moon at 10:56 P.M. (Eastern Daylight Time) on July 20, 1969. On Earth, half a billion people watched his historic first steps on television.

Armstrong started flying planes as a young man, earning his pilot's license before his driver's license. After serving in the U.S. Navy, he became a test pilot, then, in 1962, an astronaut. Armstrong's first space flight was in *Gemini 8* on March 16, 1966, which was the first piloted craft to dock with another. Unfortunately, just 30 minutes later, the spacecraft spun out of control, and Armstrong had to end the mission and return to Earth early.

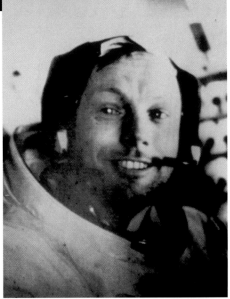

About to take his first walk on the Moon, *Edwin "Buzz" Aldrin (above) descends the ladder of the Apollo 11 lunar module, called the Eagle. Neil Armstrong (right), commander of Apollo 11, was the first person to step on the Moon.*

Armstrong's next mission was as commander of *Apollo 11*, the first piloted spacecraft to land on the Moon. Armstrong, with help from Buzz Aldrin, successfully guided the lunar module *Eagle* to a soft landing in an area called the Sea of Tranquility. The two astronauts radioed information about the powdery surface, planted an American flag, talked with President Nixon, collected rocks, and set up experiments. They climbed back into the *Eagle* after spending more than two hours outside the vehicle. In total, they spent 21 hours and 36 minutes on the Moon before rejoining astronaut Michael Collins in the command module orbiting the Moon for the return to Earth.

pads settled into the Moon's dusty surface.

Armstrong and Aldrin spent 21 hours and 36 minutes on the Moon. They worked outside the *Eagle* for more than two hours. They planted an American flag and a plaque proclaiming "We came in peace for all mankind," but did not claim the Moon as American territory. They talked with U.S. president Richard M. Nixon, set up experiments, and gathered 20 kilograms (44 pounds) of moon rocks and dirt.

On July 21, 1969, the two astronauts blasted off in the top portion of the *Eagle*. They docked with the command module and climbed inside. Then they released the *Eagle* and left it to orbit the Moon before heading back to Earth. *Apollo 11* splashed down safely in the Pacific Ocean on July 24, 1969. After *Apollo 11*, six more piloted flights headed for the Moon. Only one failed to make it—*Apollo 13*. The Apollo program ended in 1972 with the return of *Apollo 17*. SEE ALSO ARMSTRONG, NEIL.

Armstrong left the astronaut program after *Apollo 11* but continued to work for NASA for two more years. Then he became a professor of aerospace engineering at the University of Cincinnati in Cincinnati, Ohio. SEE ALSO ALDRIN, EDWIN; APOLLO PROGRAM.

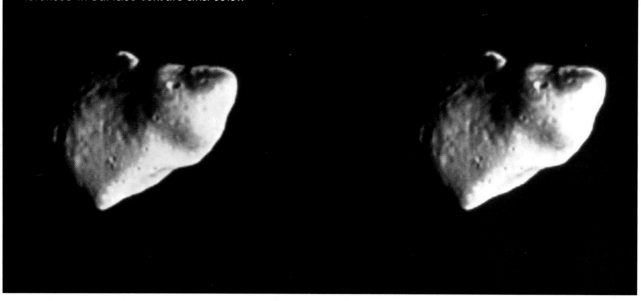

These two views of the asteroid Gaspra were taken by the Galileo spacecraft in October 1991. The image on the left shows this 19-by-12-by-11-kilometer (12-by-7.4-by-7-mile) object in approximately true colors. The image on the right shows Gaspra in exaggerated colors to bring out small differences in surface texture and color.

Asteroids

On March 23, 1989, a rocky visitor from space skimmed past Earth at a distance of less than 700,000 kilometers (420,000 miles). If the timing had been just a few hours' different, some scientists say, this chunk of rock might have collided with our world—and changed it forever.

The visitor was an asteroid, named 4581 Asclepius by astronomers. Asteroids are chunks of rock and metal that orbit the Sun. Scientists estimate that there are over 1 million asteroids, but only about 8,000 have been identified. Most of these are more than 10 kilometers (6 miles) across. The ones yet to be discovered are probably no more than 1 kilometer (half a mile) wide. Asclepius was about 300 meters (990 feet) in size. Nobody knew of Asclepius's existence before its close brush with Earth.

If an asteroid—even a small one—struck Earth, there would be long-lasting effects. An asteroid about 10 kilometers (6 miles) wide would make an enormous crater on Earth and destroy everything around it. It would fill the sky with dust and start fires, tidal waves, and floods. Such an asteroid may indeed have struck Earth 65 million years ago, wiping out the dinosaurs. (Some scientists, however, blame a comet for that ancient extinction.)

What are the chances an asteroid will hit Earth? No one knows for sure. There are hundreds of asteroids that cross Earth's orbit. One of them will make a very close pass in 2028. By then we may have the ability to blow up or change the path of an asteroid to stop it from hitting our planet. In the meantime, the United States Near-Earth Asteroid Tracking program is keeping an eye on the sky, scanning the heavens for comets and asteroids.

Most asteroids orbit the Sun far from Earth in an area lying between Mars and Jupiter called the asteroid belt. They travel counterclockwise in nearly circular paths like the planets, taking from three to six years to orbit the Sun.

Asteroids are leftover bits from the formation of the solar system that never came together to form a planet or moon as did other chunks of rock and

The asteroid Ida is nearly three times the size of Gaspra. Its tiny moon, Dactyl (far right), is only about 1.6 kilometers (1 mile) long and orbits Ida at a distance of 100 kilometers (62 miles). Like Ida and Gaspra, Dactyl is heavily cratered.

metal. Scientists think Jupiter's powerful gravity prevented them from coming together, and it may also have hurled many asteroids out of the solar system.

Today, Jupiter's gravity still pulls asteroids from the belt or kicks them into new orbits. Some travel in Jupiter's own orbital path, just in front of or behind the planet. Some orbit closer to the Sun than Earth. Others orbit beyond Saturn.

If all the asteroids in the asteroid belt were massed together, they would form an object only half the size of our Moon. The biggest asteroid is Ceres. It is about 918 kilometers (570 miles) wide.

Most asteroids are made of dark rock rich in carbon. A smaller number are a mixture of rock and metal, mostly iron. A few are a mixture of the metals iron and nickel. Rarest of all are asteroids that resemble lava rocks. Scientists figure out what asteroids are made of by studying the color of light reflecting off them. They are also able to study tiny pieces of asteroids found on Earth called meteorites. Meteorites are bits of rock from asteroids, comets, the Moon, or Mars that have landed on Earth.

The biggest asteroids are round. Smaller asteroids have odd shapes. Hektor looks like two eggs placed end to end. Eros looks like a corncob. Some asteroids even have their own moons!

Gaspra is the first asteroid to be seen close-up: The spacecraft *Galileo* photographed it in 1991. It is about 19 kilometers

(12 miles) wide. On February 17, 1996, the United States launched the spacecraft *NEAR* (Near-Earth Asteroid Rendezvous). It flew near the asteroid Eros and began orbiting it in February 2000.

Finding asteroids is not as simple in real life as it seems in movies. When a spaceship in a movie travels through an asteroid belt, it dodges and weaves to avoid rocks in its path. In the real asteroid belt, however, the rocks are few and far between. The spacecraft *Pioneer 10* spent seven months in 1972–1973 traveling in the asteroid belt. During all that time, it never met an asteroid—not even one the size of a marble. SEE ALSO COMETS; JUPITER; PHOBOS AND DEIMOS; PIONEER PROGRAM; METEOROIDS; SOLAR SYSTEM.

ASTEROIDS Facts on the Five Largest

Name	Ceres	Pallas	Vesta	Hygiea	Davida
Diameter in kilometers	918 (570 miles)	522 (324 miles)	500 (311 miles)	430 (267 miles)	336 (209 miles)
Distance from Sun in million kilometers	413.9 (257.2 million miles)	414.5 (257.6 million miles)	353.4 (219.6 million miles)	470.3 (292.2 million miles)	475.4 (295.4 million miles)
Orbital Period (years)	4.61	4.61	3.63	5.59	5.67
Year Discovered	1801	1802	1807	1849	1903
Discoverer	G. Piazzi	H. Olbers	H. Olbers	A. De Gasparis	R. Dugan

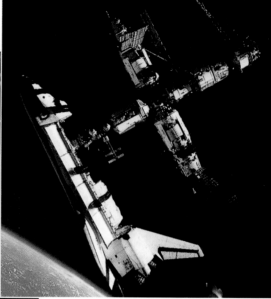

After the first docking of an American space shuttle with the space station Mir in 1995, Russian and American astronauts enjoyed a singalong in the cabin of the space station.

Astronauts and Cosmonauts

They can play catch with floating balls of orange juice. They can move objects weighing hundreds of pounds with just one finger. They sleep with air jets blowing in their faces to push away the carbon dioxide they breathe out. They are astronauts and cosmonauts, the people who fly missions into space. (*Cosmonaut* is the Russian word for astronaut.)

Astronauts' and cosmonauts' jobs were created in the late 1950s when the "space race" began between the United States and the Soviet Union. Each nation competed to achieve space "firsts."

On April 12, 1961, cosmonaut Yuri Gagarin became the first person to travel in space. He orbited the Earth once. Two years later, cosmonaut Valentina Tereshkova became the first woman in space. She orbited Earth for three days. In 1965 cosmonaut Alexei Leonov was the first person to walk in space: He spent nearly 23 minutes outside his spacecraft while in space. In 1969 the United States became the first (and only nation, so far) to land astronauts on the Moon when Neil Armstrong and Buzz Aldrin touched down on July 20th.

One question astronauts are often asked is: What experience do you need to become an astro-naut? The answer has changed over time. In 1959, for example, the National Aeronautics and Space Administration (NASA) needed astronauts for the Mercury program, which would send the first piloted U.S. spacecraft into Earth orbit. The people chosen were America's first astronauts. NASA wanted test pilots only. Test pilots were military men who flew high-speed experimental jets.

Of the 508 men who applied to be part of the Mercury program, only 39 went through NASA's tough testing program. Just seven became astronauts—the famous "Mercury 7": Scott Carpenter, Gordon Cooper, John Glenn, Virgil Grissom, Walter Schirra, Alan Shepard, and Donald Slayton.

By the end of the Apollo program in 1972, space flight had opened up to people who were not pilots. One of the astronauts aboard *Apollo 17*, the last Apollo mission, was a scientist.

Today, astronauts travel on the space shuttle instead of in space capsules. Modern astronauts may be pilots, scientists, or engineers. There are also different kinds of astronauts. Pilot astronauts can be very hard work getting where you want to go.

Astronauts prepare for weightlessness by working underwater while wearing space suits. Astronauts in training also spend time in a special jet that lets them experience weightlessness. This jet flies almost 11 kilometers (36,000 feet) high, then plunges toward Earth. During this nosedive, the astronauts experience about 20 seconds of zero gravity. They float inside the jet, bouncing off its padded walls.

Astronauts also learn how to scuba-dive, use parachutes, and survive in the wild. And learning doesn't stop when an astronaut blasts into space. Astronauts must get used to living in space. They have to be strapped in to sleep. Water does not flow, so sweat sticks to their bodies and forms puddles! Astronauts wash up by spreading water on their bodies with sponges, where it lies like a layer of jelly. Then they mop it off with towels. Eating, brushing teeth, and going to the bathroom demand special tools and skills.

Astronaut Shannon Lucid (above) spent 188 days in the Russian space station Mir in 1996, more time in space than any other American. Mark Lee (left) floated above clouds in 1994 while testing a jetpack.

are crew members who actually fly the shuttle. They must have experience flying high-speed jets and a college degree in science or engineering. They must also be in top physical condition. Mission specialists are astronauts who work with the pilot astronauts and keep track of the work carried out on the shuttle. Payload specialists are scientists and engineers who do research while on the shuttle.

Becoming an astronaut or cosmonaut takes years of training. Today's astronauts start out by studying math and science. They must work for three years in a job related to the subjects they studied. If they want to be pilot astronauts, they must have spent at least 1,000 hours in training as jet pilots. Astronauts must also be in good health and be able to work well with others.

Those who pass the tests can then enter astronaut training. They practice flying in an artificial shuttle called a simulator. They learn how to use a long robot arm to pick up and move satellites in space. They learn how to work without gravity while wearing space suits. In zero gravity, astronauts float weightlessly. It looks like a lot of fun, but it

Many astronauts have made headlines since the Moon missions. Sally Ride, a physicist, became the first American woman in space on June 18, 1983 when she flew on the shuttle *Challenger*. Mission Specialist Guion Bluford became the first African-American astronaut when he flew on the *Challenger* mission that was launched on August 30, 1983. Mae Jemison became the first African-American woman in space in 1992 when she flew on the shuttle *Endeavour*. John Glenn, who in 1962 was the first American astronaut to orbit Earth, became the oldest astronaut in space when he flew on the shuttle *Discovery* in 1998 at the age of 77. SEE ALSO ALDRIN, EDWIN; ARMSTRONG, NEIL; EXPLORATION OF THE SOLAR SYSTEM; GAGARIN, YURI; GLENN, JOHN; RIDE, SALLY.

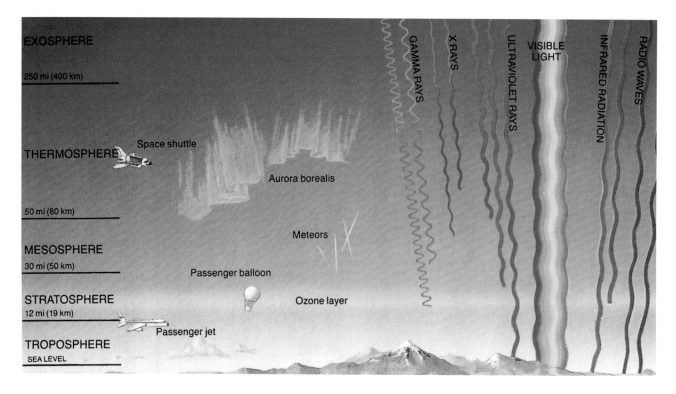

EXOSPHERE

250 mi (400 km)

THERMOSPHERE — Space shuttle

Aurora borealis

50 mi (80 km)

MESOSPHERE
30 mi (50 km)

Meteors

Passenger balloon

STRATOSPHERE
12 mi (19 km)

Ozone layer

Passenger jet

TROPOSPHERE
SEA LEVEL

GAMMA RAYS

X RAYS

ULTRAVIOLET RAYS

VISIBLE LIGHT

INFRARED RADIATION

RADIO WAVES

Atmosphere

An atmosphere is a layer of gases surrounding a planet. It is held close to the planet by gravity.

Earth's atmosphere has six main layers. The layer that supports life is the troposphere. Most clouds float within this layer. Jets fly at its top.

Plants and animals depend on the oxygen in our atmosphere. Without it, almost all life on Earth would die out. But oxygen forms only about 21 percent of the air. This is just the right amount. Any less and many life forms could not survive. Any more, and fierce fires would often break out.

Most of our air is made up of nitrogen—about 78 percent. The remaining 1 percent is made up of other gases, such as argon, carbon dioxide, helium, and ozone. Ozone is a special form of oxygen that forms a thin layer in the stratosphere, about 22 kilometers (13.7 miles) above Earth's surface. The ozone layer stops much of the Sun's ultraviolet radiation.

The atmospheres of Mars and Venus are mostly carbon dioxide. Venus's atmosphere contains thick clouds of sulfuric acid. Sunlight is absorbed by Venus's thick atmosphere and heats its surface, but the heat cannot escape, so Venus is superhot.

Earth's atmosphere is thick enough to stop most radiation harmful to life from reaching the planet's surface. The atmosphere is also thin enough so that it doesn't trap too much heat.

The gas giant planets (Jupiter, Saturn, Uranus, and Neptune) have deep atmospheres that consist mostly of hydrogen and helium, with clouds of ammonia, methane, and water. They are very different from the atmospheres of the terrestrial, or rocky, planets (Mercury, Venus, Earth, Mars, and Pluto).

Atmospheres formed after the planets did. The new planets were still hot after they formed 4.6 billion years ago. Earth, for example, did not have an atmosphere until at least 4 million years after it formed. This atmosphere was made of gases that leaked out of the Earth's rocky surface as it cooled. Other gases were belched out by volcanoes. Earth's early atmosphere included nitrogen, carbon dioxide, methane, and water vapor. Later, plants growing in the oceans added oxygen to the mix.

The gas giants hold lots of hydrogen in their atmospheres. Earth, Venus, and Mars do not because hydrogen is a very light gas. The terrestrial planets' gravity was too weak to stop it from flying off into space. The warmth of these planets also heated the hydrogen, making it escape even faster. The gas giants' gravity was strong. The gas giants were also far from the Sun and cold, so they hung on to their sluggish, chilly molecules of hydrogen.

The Moon is small and has weak gravity—so it has no atmosphere to speak of. However, some moons do have atmospheres. Titan, Saturn's biggest moon, is the only moon known to have a thick atmosphere.

In 1996, the Hubble Space Telescope discovered thin wisps of oxygen surrounding Jupiter's moons Ganymede and Europa. Scientists think the oxygen comes from water ice on the moons' surfaces. Sunlight, meteor strikes, and electrically charged particles may be kicking oxygen atoms out of the water molecules. The *Galileo* spacecraft found that the moon Callisto has a thin carbon dioxide atmosphere, and that the atmosphere of the moon Io holds sulfur dioxide. *See also Gas Giant Planets; Moons of the Planets; Terrestrial Planets.*

Aurora

An aurora looks like a flickering curtain of colored light glowing in the sky. Auroras dance over areas that are very far north or very far south on Earth. Auroras in the north are called the aurora borealis, or the northern lights. Those in the south are called the aurora australis, or the southern lights.

Auroras are caused by charged particles flowing from the Sun. This flow is called the solar wind. Earth's magnetic field forces the solar wind to flow toward its north and south poles, where the charged particles hit gas atoms in the upper atmosphere and cause them to glow. *See also Solar Wind; Sun.*

Black Hole

A black hole is an object that may be formed when a star at least 20 times bigger than the Sun dies. After burning all its fuel, a dying star collapses as gravity compresses it into a tightly packed bundle much smaller than the original star. A small black hole may have about 10 times the mass of our Sun, but all squashed into an unbelievably dense ball perhaps only about 60 kilometers (95 miles) wide. A tablespoon would weigh a billion tons.

A black hole is not only dense but also totally black! Its gravity is so incredibly strong even light cannot escape from it. X rays, heat waves, and radio waves are trapped in a black hole, too, so scientists cannot learn about black holes from their radiation.

Black holes reveal clues about themselves by the way they make other space objects behave, however. A black hole's strong gravity makes any star orbiting close by go very fast. It may pull matter from the orbiting star. This matter can produce X rays before disappearing into the black hole.

Astronomers have found what may be a huge black hole at the center of our galaxy. Some say this black hole has a mass of one million Suns.

A black hole causes very weird things to happen near it. A spacecraft approaching a black hole would appear to an observer far away to be standing still even though it was actually moving. The spacecraft would be ripped apart as it fell in the black hole, and then crushed. Scientists are using whatever information they can collect to come up with new theories about other strange effects black holes may create. *See also Galaxy; Star.*

A black hole pulls gas *from the atmosphere of an orange-red star in this painting. The gas gives off X rays as it spirals into the invisible black hole.*

Callisto

Callisto is one of Jupiter's four biggest moons. (All four were discovered by the astronomer Galileo in 1610 and are known as the Galilean moons.) Callisto is more heavily cratered than any other object in the solar system. The craters date back to the beginning of the solar system, when asteroids and meteorites bombed the newly formed planets and moons. On Callisto's icy surface, these impacts created flat craters with ripples around them. Dark dust kicked up by the impacts settled like soot on the ground. Melted water flowed into the craters and froze. This made the craters more shallow than craters on moons with rocky surfaces. There are no wide plains as there are on our Moon.

Callisto's surface is the oldest yet discovered in the solar system, and it has not changed much in the 4 billion years since most of the craters were formed. This lack of activity is unusual for a moon of Callisto's size. Its diameter of about 4,800 kilo-meters (2,983 miles) makes it the third largest moon in the solar system. It is about twice the size of our Moon and has a thin carbon-dioxide atmosphere.

Callisto is the darkest Galilean moon, yet it reflects light twice as well as our Moon. Its most vivid feature is Valhalla, a crater with a center 300 kilometers (186 miles) wide. Rings around it extend out 1,500 kilometers (930 miles) from its center.

The spacecraft *Galileo* measured changes in Callisto's gravitational field as it flew past Jupiter in 1996 and 1997. It discovered that Callisto is made of ice and rock mixed together, with more rock toward the middle. Callisto is the farthest away of Jupiter's large moons. It has not been tugged by the giant planet's gravity as much the others. As a result, Callisto's interior has not heated up, melted, and separated into several layers like those in the other Galilean moons. There could be, however, at least one distinct layer—an ocean beneath the thick icy crust that covers the planet. SEE ALSO EUROPA; GANYMEDE; IO; JUPITER; PLANETS OF THE SOLAR SYSTEM.

Impact rings surrounding the crater Valhalla on Callisto cover an area 3,000 kilometers (1,860 miles) wide. Callisto's frigid surface consists of rocks and ice, which is as hard as stone at Callisto's surface temperature of -145°C (-230°F).

Cape Canaveral

Cape Canaveral, located on an island off the east coast of central Florida, is home to the Kennedy Space Center and the Cape Canaveral Air Station. Cape Canaveral was called "Cape Kennedy" from 1963 to 1973, when its name was officially switched back to Canaveral.

The Kennedy Space Center is operated by the National Aeronautics and Space Administration (NASA). It covers about 34,000 hectares (84,000 acres) of land and includes shuttle launch pads, a runway, office buildings, museums, a wildlife refuge, and the huge Vehicle Assembly Building, where space shuttles are prepared for launch. It is named in honor of President John F. Kennedy, who in 1961 vowed to put a man on the Moon by 1970.

Cape Canaveral is a good launch site. It usually enjoys clear weather and is near the ocean, so discarded rocket stages fall safely into water.

Ceres

Ceres is the largest known asteroid. It is about 918 kilometers (570 miles) wide. If all the asteroids orbiting the Sun were clumped together, they would form an object less than half the size of Earth's Moon. Ceres would make up almost half of that small object. Ceres is part of the asteroid belt between Mars and Jupiter. It travels around the Sun at a distance of about 414 million kilometers (257 million miles).

Ceres is also the first asteroid ever viewed from Earth. It was discovered on January 1, 1801, by Giuseppe Piazzi. Piazzi was studying the sky to find the "missing planet" that was believed to exist between Mars and Jupiter. He noticed a point of light in the sky that didn't appear on an official list of stars. Over the next few nights, he saw that it had moved. At first he thought he had found a planet or a comet. Then he found two more of these odd objects and realized he was looking at something new. Piazzi had discovered asteroids, the "minor planets" of the solar system. *SEE ALSO ASTEROIDS.*

Charon

In 1978, astronomer James Christy was peering at a photograph of Pluto taken through a telescope in Arizona when he noticed a bump on the planet that made it look like a one-eared Mickey Mouse. The bump turned out to be a moon. This moon, named Charon, is Pluto's only satellite.

Charon is half the size of Pluto. No other moon is so large in comparison to the planet it orbits. Charon orbits Pluto at a distance of only 19,400 kilometers (12,000 miles). It always has the same side turned toward Pluto. Likewise, Pluto always shows the same side to Charon. They are locked in what is called "mutual synchronous spin." This means Charon orbits Pluto once in the same amount of time it takes Pluto to spin around once—6.4 days. Charon doesn't rise and set in Pluto's sky as the Moon does in Earth's sky. It stays in the same spot.

Most scientists think that Charon and Pluto are really a double planet. Some scientists believe that Charon may be a chunk of rock that was knocked out of Pluto. *SEE ALSO MOONS OF THE PLANETS; PLUTO.*

Comets

Comets are "dirty snowballs"—chunks of ice and rock traveling around the Sun in long, elliptical orbits. The ice is frozen water and frozen gases; the rock contains bits of metal and other minerals. Comets are also "time capsules" because they give us a view of the past. Most astronomers believe that comets were made from the material that was left over after our solar system formed 4.6 billion years ago.

Comets may even have helped start life on Earth. They contain water, carbon, and other chemical building blocks of living things. Some scientists think comets showered the early Earth with these ingredients necessary for life.

One comet, however, may have destroyed millions of Earth's living things. Many scientists believe that a comet smashed into the Earth near the Yucatan Peninsula in Mexico 65 million years ago, causing skies to fill with dust and killing most plant and animal life—including the dinosaurs.

Countless comets exist on the fringes of the solar system. Some are in a wide band called the Kuiper Belt, an area stretching from Neptune to beyond Pluto and containing bits from the solar system's birth. Other comets may exist in the Oort Cloud, a huge mass of material surrounding our solar system. A comet can fall into an orbit that brings it closer to the Sun when it it is pulled by the gravity of a large object.

Some comets are called short-period comets because they orbit the Sun once every 200 years or less. Halley's comet, which streaks past Earth every 76 years, is a short-period comet. Long-period comets take over 200 years to orbit the Sun. Comet Hale-Bopp, which blazed the brightest across Earth's skies in 1997, is estimated to return in 2,380 years. Others take 100,000 years or more to orbit. Still others shoot off into interstellar space.

Comet Hale-Bopp displays its twin tails over Arizona. The long blue tail is made of gases; the white tail is dust. Alan Hale and Thomas Bopp discovered the comet separately in 1995.

A comet's solid body is called the nucleus. It is a chunk of rock, metal, gases, and ices of chemical compounds, such as water, ammonia and methane. In 1986, the spacecraft *Giotto* flew within 600 kilometers (375 miles) of the nucleus of Halley's comet and photographed it. The pictures showed a jet-black, lumpy object about 16 kilometers (10 miles) long and 8 kilometers (5 miles) wide.

As a comet gets closer to the Sun, its ice begins to melt, releasing gases and dust that form a huge cloud of vapor called a coma around the remaining nucleus. Together, the coma and nucleus make up the head of the comet. The solar wind—a gust of tiny, fast, electrically charged particles pouring from the Sun—blows some of the coma into a magnificent tail that may stream hundreds of millions of miles into space. The solar wind pushes the tail behind the comet as it approaches the Sun and in front of the comet as it travels away from the Sun. A yellowish-white, curved tail is made of dust and is usually shorter than the bluish, straight tail, which is composed of gases. A comet may have a dust tail, a gas tail, or both. We can see comets because the dust in their comas and tails reflects sunlight and because sunlight makes the gases shine.

Once people blamed comets for killing kings, bringing sickness, and causing armies to lose wars. Even in 1910, many people believed that if Earth passed through the tail of Halley's comet, they would inhale poisonous gases and die. Today we know that passing through the remains of a comet's tail brings only a beautiful display of shooting stars (called meteor showers) in the sky. *SEE ALSO HALLEY'S COMET; KUIPER BELT; METEOROIDS; OORT CLOUD.*

COSMIC CRASH:

The Story of Comet Shoemaker-Levy 9

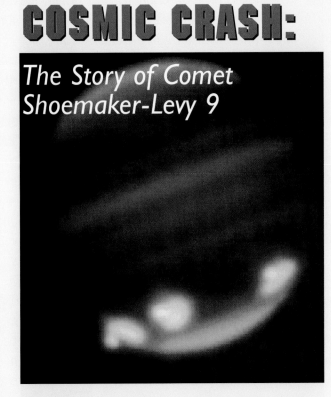

Huge fireballs exploded on Jupiter *as chunks of Comet Shoemaker-Levy 9 slammed into the planet in 1994. Some fireballs were much larger than Earth.*

When astronomers Eugene and Carolyn Shoemaker and David Levy first spotted a comet in a photograph taken through a telescope in March 1993, they may have suspected it was to have an historic impact. As they studied the new comet—now named after them—the astronomers discovered that it was broken into at least 20 chunks. While in its orbit around Jupiter, the comet had come too close to the giant planet and was pulled apart by its powerful gravity. The pieces continued to orbit the planet.

In July 1994, the pull of the Sun's gravity altered the orbit of the comet pieces, causing them to smash into Jupiter at about 210,000 kilometers (130,000 miles) per hour). Spectacular fiery explosions resulted, and huge dark marks were left in the planet's atmosphere. Comet Shoemaker-Levy 9 is no more, but its astronomical fame will last forever as the first cosmic collision to be observed and recorded.

The constellation Orion is famous for its row of three bright stars. The ancient Greeks imagined them as the belt of Orion, the Hunter. But the Mayas saw them as parts of a turtle's shell.

Greeks thought the Great Bear resembled a hunting goddess named Callisto in disguise. The Romans called the Big Dipper Septentriones, which means "seven plowing oxen." Europeans call this group of stars within Ursa Major the Plow or the Wagon.

What constellations you see depends on your location and the time of year. You will see different constellations in the northern sky than a person in the southern hemisphere sees. For example, the Little Dipper (which contains the North Star) is easily viewed at northern latitudes, while the Southern Cross is visible only as far north as Key West, Florida.

Stars in constellations are named after their constellations. For example, the bright red star Betelgeuse is also called Alpha Orionis, indicating that it lies in Orion. SEE ALSO NORTH STAR; STAR.

Copernicus, Nicolaus

Nicolaus Copernicus (1473–1543) was a Polish astronomer and one of the first scientists to state that Earth orbits the Sun.

Five hundred years ago, most people believed that Earth stood still, did not spin, and did not orbit the Sun. Instead, they thought Earth was surrounded by transparent spheres that rotated; inside each sphere was the Sun, Moon, or a planet.

There was a problem with this idea, however. Mars, Jupiter, and Saturn sometimes seemed to move backward. To explain this strange behavior of the planets, astronomers supposed that there was a system of circles within circles.

Copernicus had a different explanation. He argued that Earth spins once a day on an

Copernicus died over 150 years before his theories were widely accepted.

Constellations

A constellation is a pattern formed by stars in the night sky. The stars in a constellation are not actually close together; some may be much nearer Earth than others. Humans have long used their imaginations to link stars and form dot-to-dot pictures. There are 88 constellations in all, each named for an ancient god, goddess, animal, or object.

Ursa Major, or the Great Bear, for example, is the constellation containing the familiar group of seven stars called the Big Dipper. The ancient imaginary pole that runs through its middle called the axis. At the same time, he said, Earth travels around the Sun once a year. He also said that the other planets move around the Sun. Copernicus still believed each celestial body was embedded in a sphere, but he solved many problems by assuming that Earth moved.

Copernicus's ideas helped other astronomers figure out how the universe works. Some of the famous astronomers inspired by Copernicus were Johannes Kepler, Galileo, and Sir Isaac Newton. *See also Galileo; Kepler, Johannes; Newton, Sir Isaac; Ptolemy.*

Crater

A crater is a big hole in the surface of a moon or planet. An impact crater is created by a meteorite or asteroid crashing into the surface. A very big crater surrounded by mountains or rings is called an impact basin.

Craters help scientists figure out what a planet or moon is made of. Objects that hit Jupiter's moon Callisto, for example, created bright white craters by exposing ice under Callisto's dark brown surface.

Scientists also study the materials, called ejecta, that fly out from a crater when it is formed. On Earth, scientists have found ejecta nearly 484 kilometers (300 miles) away from the Chicxulub Crater near the Yucatan Peninsula of Mexico. Such clues help scientists piece together the details of an ancient crash. In this case, the crash happened 65 million years ago and may have wiped out the dinosaurs.

Craters also tell us a lot about a planet or moon's history. Mercury, for example, is covered with craters. Its surface dates back to the beginning of the solar system, more than 4 billion years ago when millions of asteroids and meteorites smashed into the new planets. We know that Mercury's surface is very old because it still bears the evidence of these ancient impacts. We also know that Mercury's volcanoes were extinct at this time because they did not fill the craters with lava.

Weather has worn away many craters on Venus, Earth, and Mars. Lava from volcanoes has filled others. When the surface of a planet or moon has only a few craters or none at all, it may mean the surface has changed a lot over time. It may also mean the surface is young. Venus, for example, has fewer than a thousand impact craters. Scientists believe its surface is only about 500 million years old.

Some moons are heavily cratered in just a few areas. The moon Enceladus, which orbits Saturn, is one such moon. It has many craters in one half and hardly any in the other. Scientists have noticed canals in the moon's icy surface, too. They think slush may have flowed in these canals. This slush may have filled up some craters but not others.

Earth still has some ancient craters. There is a crater 81 kilometers (50 miles) wide in Chesapeake Bay. Arizona boasts Barringer Meteor Crater, which is 1,265 meters (4,150 feet) wide. A chain of five craters stretches across parts of Europe and North America. Another chain of eight craters runs from Illinois to Kansas. Scientists have found about 160 craters so far, and there may be many others beneath the sea. *See also Mercury; Moon.*

Copernicus Crater, 93 kilometers (58 miles) wide, is one of the Moon's youngest impact craters. Only large impact craters have central mountains.

Earth's very thin crust floats on the upper mantle (red), a layer of partially molten (melted) rock. Currents in the upper mantle slowly move the continents around. The next layer down is the lower mantle (orange), also made of molten rock. Next to the core is the outer core (yellow), a layer of molten metal where electrical currents create Earth's magnetic field. At the center (white) is the inner core of solid iron and nickel.

Earth

Earth is a blue sphere streaked with white, gleaming in the darkness of space. In some photographs taken from space, the entire planet seems to be one big ocean. This view is not far from the truth. Water covers three-fourths of Earth. "Ocean" would be a more logical name for our planet! It is the only planet with liquid surface water.

Earth's vast oceans keep air temperatures within a steady range by storing huge amounts of the Sun's heat. Oceans cool down the air by soaking up heat and warm up the air by releasing heat.

Oceans also play a key role in Earth's never-ending water cycle. Water vapor rising from oceans forms clouds that drop rain onto the land, rivers, lakes, ponds, and oceans.

Water vapor forms a small portion of Earth's atmosphere. This vapor, together with gases such as carbon dioxide, traps heat created when the Sun's light warms the land and sea and holds it in like a blanket. Along with the oceans, the atmosphere keeps temperatures from changing drastically.

Earth's atmosphere is made up of 78 percent nitrogen, 21 percent oxygen, and 1 percent argon, carbon dioxide, and other gases. This oxygen level is just right for supporting life as we know it. Plants give off oxygen as they use sunlight and absorb carbon dioxide to make the food they need. This process is called photosynthesis. Over 80 percent of all photosynthesis takes place in the oceans.

About 22 kilometers (14 miles) high in the atmosphere floats a chemical compound called ozone. It prevents dangerous amounts of the Sun's ultraviolet rays from reaching the ground. Ultraviolet rays are harmful to living things.

Fortunately, Earth's gravity is strong enough to hang onto its protective atmosphere. Otherwise, Earth might be like the Moon, which has no atmosphere because its gravity is weak.

Earth's surface is shaped by forces that start deep inside it at its core. The core has two parts: a solid iron-nickel inner portion and a liquid metal outer portion. Currents in this liquid portion produce electricity and give Earth its magnetic field.

The outer core is red-hot—about 4,100°C (7,400°F). It heats the layers of rock above it, the lower and the upper mantles. The upper mantle is partially melted rock. Floating on the mantle is Earth's outer shell, which is broken into big pieces, called plates. These plates drift slowly on the mantle like puzzle pieces in molasses. This motion is called plate tectonics.

Earth's tilt causes seasons *and days of varying length. If Earth's axis did not tilt, there would not be seasons; days would be the same length. If Earth were tilted 90 degrees, one side would have daylight for half a year while the other would be in darkness.*

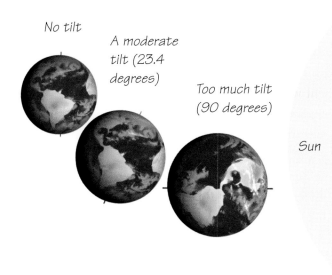

No tilt

A moderate tilt (23.4 degrees)

Too much tilt (90 degrees)

Sun

EARTH Fast Facts

Mass: 1 x Earth
Volume: 1 x Earth
Diameter at equator: 12,756 kilometers (7,926 miles). Fifth largest planet
Distance from Sun: 149.6 million kilometers (93 million miles). Third planet from Sun
Moons: 1
Average temperature: 15°C (59°F)
Time to rotate on axis: 23 hours, 56 minutes
Time to orbit Sun: 365.26 days
Rings: No
Atmosphere: Nitrogen, oxygen

DID YOU KNOW? Water covers three-fourths of the Earth's surface.

Just 200 million years ago, a big land mass containing all of today's continents broke up. The pieces slowly spread across the globe and are still drifting today. Earthquakes rumble when plates collide or slip past each other. Volcanoes erupt where plates meet. Hot molten rock gushes up from the mantle under the ocean along ridges, pushing the sea floor apart.

All this repaving of Earth has erased most craters left by comets, asteroids, and meteorites in the past. But a few still exist. One of them is Barringer Meteor Crater in Arizona, a giant hole made in the desert 49,000 years ago.

Without its oceans and atmosphere, Earth would not support life as we know it. So far, Earth is the only planet in the solar system known to have life. Life on Earth may have started deep in the ocean. The ocean floor is home to strange worms, bacteria, and other creatures. They cluster around tall, rocky stacks called black smokers from which water bubbles out that is hot enough to burn skin. Life survives here without photosynthesis.

Scientists don't know if life exists on other planets—but discoveries made in Earth's own ocean may someday help them find out. SEE ALSO ATMOSPHERE; LIFE; MAGNETIC FIELDS; MOON; SEASONS; TIDES; WATER.

Albert Einstein carried out some of his greatest experiments in his head rather than in a laboratory and left it to other scientists to prove his theories.

Einstein, Albert

Albert Einstein (1879–1955) was a physicist whose ideas about energy, motion, space, light, gravity, and time changed the study of outer space forever.

Einstein's special theory of relativity states that measurements of space and time may not be the same for different observers. A measurement of space or time changes depending on the speed and direction of an observer's motion.

In 1915, Einstein published a general theory of relativity, which dealt with gravity and time in space. In part, this theory states that big objects like the Sun cause space to curve. Smaller objects, like the planets, follow these curves and thus orbit the Sun. Einstein said that light could even be forced to curve. In 1919, Einstein's prediction was shown to be true during a solar eclipse. Scientists studying the eclipse were able to see that starlight was bent by the Sun's gravity.

In 1921, Einstein won the Nobel Prize for his ideas about light. Einstein's work stated that light did not just travel in waves. It also could exist as light particles, called photons.

Einstein's theories led to some of the technology we use every day, and they are important to scientists studying light and objects moving near the speed of light. Scientists investigating black holes, exploding stars, and other events in space use Einstein's theories, too. So do scientists studying particles smaller than atoms. *SEE ALSO SOLAR ECLIPSE.*

Albert Einstein carried out some of his greatest experiments in his head rather than in a laboratory and left it to other scientists to prove his theories.

Erosion

Erosion is the movement of soil and rock by wind, water, and gravity. On Earth, winds whip sand and dust against rocks, scrubbing them into new shapes. Rivers cut channels through stone and move tons of soil with the water's current. Huge, flowing ribbons of ice carve valleys. Waves crash on shores, carrying sand away and piling it up elsewhere.

Erosion has erased much of Earth's early history. Earth formed about 4.6 billion years ago. Then it was blasted by objects from space until about 3.8 billion years ago. The craters from this time have disappeared. Water and wind buried them beneath rock and soil and smoothed their edges.

Meanwhile, volcanoes in Earth's crust added new surface material when they erupted and spread lava that hardened. Most of Earth's surface is only about 100 million years old or less. Scientists have found only about 160 impact craters so far on Earth, but they are fairly young as far as craters go—just a few million years old.

The Moon, on the other hand, has many craters because it has no flowing water, no atmosphere, and thus no wind. Mercury, too, lacks wind and water, and it is also heavily cratered.

Erosion's effects can be seen on Mars, however. Mars' surface shows ripples in places where water may once have flowed. Giant dust storms blow across the red planet, changing the landscape as winds chip away at the rock and carry the soil from one area to another. Dunes of dirt can be seen heaped near Mars's north pole. Wind has not scrubbed away all craters, though. Southern Mars is filled with craters because the land there is older than 3.8 billion years. The northern lands, however, formed later in the solar system's history and so have fewer craters. *SEE ALSO CRATER; EARTH; IO; MARS; MERCURY; VENUS; VOLCANOES; WATER.*

Europa

Europa is one of Jupiter's four largest moons. It is about the size of our Moon. Unlike our Moon, however, Europa is covered with ice and has few craters. Long cracks and ridges scar its surface instead.

Europa is a cold world some 780 million kilometers (490 million miles) from the Sun. Surface temperatures average only −145°C (−230°F). Yet scientists think Europa is one of the most likely places to find extraterrestrial life in the solar system.

Why Europa? Its frozen crust does not seem friendly to life. But many scientists think that this smooth, cracked surface may hide a deep ocean of water or slushy ice, which could contain life.

The spacecraft *Galileo* helped gather important clues about Europa's surface and what may lie beneath it. In 1997, *Galileo* photographed large areas of icy ridges and cracks that resemble the seas of Earth's poles in spring, when the ice that covers these chilly waters breaks up into sections.

Some of Europa's ridges may be places where the icy crust pulled apart, letting warm water gush up and freeze in the crack that resulted. Other ridges may have formed when sections of Europa's crust shoved against each other. "Ice volcanoes" may also have erupted in long lines, spilling icy water and dirt onto the surface.

Some scientists say Europa's lack of craters proves its surface is just a few million years old. They say it has been covered with a fresh surface again and again as water welled up from beneath the crust and then froze on top of it. Others say the surface may be much older—about a billion years old.

How could a liquid ocean exist on chilly Europa, so far from the Sun's heat? Europa may produce its own heat as its insides are pulled on by the gravity of Jupiter and other moons. Materials would rub together and make heat by friction, just as your hands heat up when you rub them together.

The United States plans to send a spacecraft to Europa in 2003 that will use radar to find out what's under Europa's ice. In the future, a probe may land on Europa and drill into its mysterious surface to unlock its secrets. *SEE ALSO GANYMEDE; JUPITER; MOONS OF THE PLANETS.*

Europa's icy surface (right) is crisscrossed by dark cracks and low, thin ridges. Beneath this frozen crust there may be an ocean of water. The two views of Europa (below) are a color-enhanced image (below, left) and a normal one (below, right). Orange and brown areas indicate rocks mixed with ice.

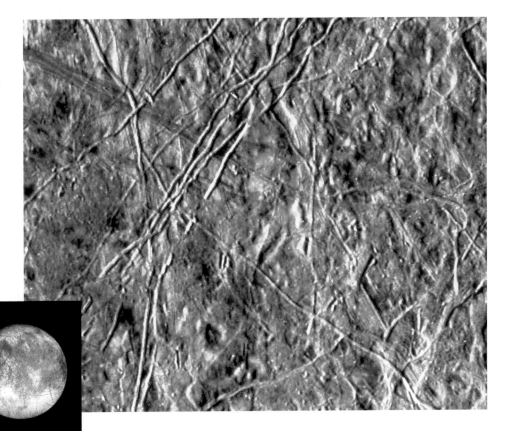

Exploration of the Solar System

The first explorers of the solar system could use only their eyes to study the skies. When telescopes were invented in the 1600s, the early space explorers began finding new marvels. Three hundred years later, more powerful telescopes helped astronomers discover galaxies beyond our own Milky Way galaxy. Beginning in 1957, humans began exploring our solar system by sending spacecraft into it.

The first space trip was made by a basketball-sized radio satellite called *Sputnik 1* on October 4, 1957. It was the first man-made satellite to orbit Earth and belonged to the Union of Soviet Socialist Republics (USSR). *Sputnik* started a "space race" between the USSR and the United States.

The United States launched its first satellite, *Explorer 1*, in January 1958. Weighing only 14 kilograms (31 pounds), *Explorer 1* studied Earth's atmosphere. In October 1958, the United States established the National Aeronautics and Space Administration (NASA) to develop America's space program.

Once satellites were orbiting Earth, scientists began setting new goals, such as sending probes to the Moon and other planets and launching humans into space and landing them on the Moon.

In January 1959, the USSR's *Luna 1* became the first spacecraft to escape Earth's gravity, though it

The Cassini spacecraft *will use its main engine as a break when it begins orbiting Saturn in 2004 to observe the planet and its rings close-up.*

failed to reach the Moon. Later that year, *Luna 2* crashed on the Moon. *Luna 3* took photographs of the Moon's far side—the side that never faces Earth. *Luna 9* landed safely on the Moon in 1966.

Meanwhile, the United States had begun sending humans into space on short flights. Seven astronauts, called the Mercury 7, trained for these missions. First, NASA launched 11 pilotless test flights. Flight number 12 went up in 1961 with a chimpanzee.

Finally, on May 5, 1961, Alan Shepard became the first American in space. He flew for only 15 minutes. The next year, John Glenn orbited Earth. Neither man was the first in space. That honor went to Yuri Gagarin of the USSR, who orbited Earth in a capsule called *Vostok 1* on April 12, 1961.

The Mercury program was followed by the Gemini program, which ran from 1964 to 1966. Mercury astronauts had gone up one at a time and had little control over their spacecraft. Gemini astronauts went up in pairs. Gemini spacecraft were designed to be controlled by astronauts and could be moved into new orbits when small rockets were fired. Gemini astronauts also could dock their capsules with other spacecraft—and even leave their craft to "walk" in space.

The Gemini program led into the Apollo program and its goal of landing humans on the Moon. On July 20, 1969, *Apollo 11* achieved this goal when Neil Armstrong and Buzz Aldrin stepped on the Moon's surface. Five more Apollo flights landed on the Moon before the Apollo program ended in 1972.

But only unpiloted spacecraft flew beyond the Moon. The USSR's *Venera 7* landed on Venus on December 15, 1970. In 1971, the United States' *Mariner 9* orbited Mars, and in 1972 *Venera 8* landed on Venus and analyzed soil samples. Then, in 1973, U.S. spacecraft *Pioneer 10* flew past Jupiter. In 1974, the U.S. *Mariner 10* zipped past Mercury.

Mars proved to be one of the most popular solar system destinations. The USSR sent seven probes to Mars from 1962 to 1971. The United States put two Viking spacecraft into orbit around Mars and landed space probes on its surface in 1976. A craft called *Pathfinder* landed on Mars in 1997 and let loose a little "Mars buggy" called *Sojourner* to explore its surface.

A new era in space exploration dawned in 1981 with the launch of the first space shuttle—the first spacecraft that could take off, orbit Earth, land on a runway, and then be used again for other missions. In 1989, a shuttle launched *Magellan*, which visited Venus and mapped its surface. A shuttle also launched *Galileo*, which flew to Jupiter to study the giant planet and its moons. The Hubble Space Telescope was released by a shuttle, too, in 1990.

The first main space project of the 21st century is the International Space Station. There have been space stations in the past. The United States had *Skylab*, which orbited Earth from 1973 to 1979. The USSR (now Russia) operated space station *Mir* from 1986 to 1999. The International Space Station will be much bigger. *Skylab* and *Mir* were about the size of a space shuttle. The new station is about the size of two football fields side-by-side. Sixteen nations, including the United States and Russia, are working together to build it.

Farther from home, spacecraft will be at work studying other parts of the solar system. *Cassini,*

The first human exploration of another planet will most likely take place on Mars sometime in the first half of the 21st century.

which was launched in October 1997, is scheduled to reach Saturn by 2004. It will study the ringed planet and drop a probe onto its moon Titan. By 2012 or shortly after, a spacecraft called the *Pluto-Kuiper Express* should arrive at Pluto—the farthest planet from the Sun. It will be the first space probe ever to visit Pluto. SEE ALSO MARINER SERIES; PIONEER PROGRAM; PLANETS OF THE SOLAR SYSTEM; SPACE STATION.

SOLAR SYSTEM EXPLORATION 20th-Century Highlights

October 4, 1957
Soviet satellite *Sputnik 1* is launched into orbit around Earth

January 2, 1959
Soviet spacecraft *Luna 1* escapes Earth's gravity

September 14, 1959
Soviet spacecraft *Luna 2* crashes on the Moon

April 12, 1961
Soviet cosmonaut Yuri Gagarin orbits Earth aboard *Vostok 2*

May 5, 1961
Astronaut Alan Shepard becomes first American in space

February 20, 1962
Astronaut John Glenn becomes the first American to orbit Earth

December 1962
U.S. spacecraft *Mariner 2* flies past Venus

July 14–15, 1965
U.S. spacecraft *Mariner 4* flies past Mars and sends back images

February 3, 1966
Soviet spacecraft *Luna 9* makes soft landing on the Moon

December 24–25, 1968
U.S. astronauts in *Apollo 8* orbit the Moon

July 20, 1969
U.S. astronauts aboard *Apollo 11* land on the Moon

December 15, 1970
Soviet spacecraft *Venera 7* lands on Venus and transmits from the surface

April 19, 1971
Soviet space station *Salyut 1* orbits Earth

November 24, 1971
U.S. spacecraft *Mariner 9* orbits Mars

December 1973
U.S. spacecraft *Pioneer 10* visits Jupiter

March 1974–March 1975
U.S. spacecraft *Mariner 10* flies past Mercury three times

July 20, 1976
U.S. spacecraft *Viking 1* makes soft landing on Mars

September 1, 1979
U.S. spacecraft *Pioneer 11* flies by Saturn

April 12, 1981
First flight of U.S. space shuttle

March 1982
Soviet spacecraft *Venera 13* and *14* sample Venus's soil

June 13, 1983
U.S. spacecraft *Pioneer 10* flies beyond Pluto

January 1986
Voyager 2 flies by Uranus

August 1989
Voyager 2 flies by Neptune

July 4, 1997
U.S. spacecraft *Mars Pathfinder* lands on Mars, where it releases a small, six-wheeled vehicle called *Sojourner*

G

Gagarin, Yuri

Yuri Gagarin (1934–1968) was the first human to be launched into space. On April 12, 1961, the Soviet cosmonaut was rocketed into space aboard the spacecraft *Vostok 1*, which consisted of an instrument section and a capsule. Gagarin rode in the capsule. The flight of *Vostok 1* was controlled by computers, but Gagarin could have piloted the spacecraft himself had there been an emergency.

Gagarin's farthest distance from Earth was 315 kilometers (203 miles). He orbited Earth once in 108 minutes. Then his history-making journey ended. The capsule and the instrument section separated, and the capsule plunged to Earth. Gagarin ejected from the capsule about 7,000 meters (23,000 feet) above Earth and floated down in a parachute. (Some Soviet officials insisted he had stayed in the capsule. Cosmonauts on later Vostok flights all used parachutes, so it's likely that Gagarin did, too.) Gagarin helped to train future cosmonauts and worked on another space program called Soyuz. A crater on the Moon is named after him. SEE ALSO ASTRONAUTS AND COSMONAUTS.

Cosmonaut Yuri Gagarin *became the first man in space when he rode once around the Earth on the Soviet spacecraft* Vostok 1 *on April 12, 1961.*

Galaxy

When you look up at the night sky, you see stars sprinkled across it. It's easy to picture the universe as being like this, too—a huge, black space with stars scattered around. But stars aren't just tossed throughout the universe. They are gathered in groups called galaxies.

A galaxy is a huge collection of stars, gas, dust, and other matter held together by gravity. All large galaxies may hold black holes in their middles. There are four main galaxy shapes: elliptical, spiral, barred spiral, and irregular.

An elliptical galaxy looks round or oval and blurry. It is full of old stars that have cooled. It does not have many clouds of dust and gas. There is no clear nucleus, or middle, to it. Over half of all known galaxies are elliptical.

A spiral galaxy has from one to four arms extending from its middle and looping around it. It looks like a pinwheel when seen from the top. The arms hold young stars and clouds of dust and gas.

A barred spiral galaxy is a kind of spiral galaxy. It has a bright stripe of stars running across its middle. The arms appear to be attached to this bright bar.

Irregular galaxies don't fit into any of these groups. They have no common pattern or shape.

Galaxies are separated by vast distances. A minor galaxy, the Sagittarius Dwarf Elliptical Galaxy, is the closest galaxy to ours, the Milky Way. It lies 50,000 light-years from Earth. (A light-year is the distance that light can travel in a vacuum in one year—about 9.46 trillion kilometers or 5.88 trillion miles.) Another neighbor of ours is the immense Andromeda galaxy. At 2.2 million light-years away, it is the farthest object you can see with the naked eye.

As stars sometimes cluster together inside galaxies, galaxies also flock together in groups called galaxy clusters. The Milky Way, Andromeda, and 28 other galaxies are all part of a cluster that is called the Local Group. The Local Group is part of an even bigger cluster called the Local Supercluster. This supercluster holds many galaxy clusters—some of which contain thousands of galaxies!

The Whirlpool Galaxy is a spiral galaxy with a smaller spiral companion to its left. The closeup of the galaxy's core (inset) shows a strange X-like area that could be the site of a black hole.

Like planets and stars, galaxies rotate. It takes a very long time for a galaxy to spin around once. For example, our solar system takes 240 million years to travel once around the center of the galaxy. Galaxies also move through the universe. They are very far apart from each other, so they have lots of room to roam. Sometimes, however, they sweep close to each other or even collide.

A galaxy called Arp 220 seems to be made up of two galaxies that collided. Like a queen ant laying eggs, Arp 220 produces new stars at a very fast pace. The Cartwheel Galaxy is circled by a huge ring of stars. This ring was caused by a crash with another galaxy. Scientists have also found extra-large galaxies that seem to swallow smaller galaxies.

Scientists haven't known about galaxies for very long. In the 1840s, an Irish astronomer discovered that an object named M51 had a spiral shape. Without knowing it, he had discovered the first spiral galaxy (called the Whirlpool Galaxy). But it wasn't until 1923 that we knew for sure that other galaxies existed. Astronomer Edwin Hubble proved this when he used a very powerful telescope to photograph what was then called the Andromeda Nebula. A nebula is a cloud of dust and gas. Hubble found a special type of star in the photograph that helped him figure out that the Andromeda Nebula was actually too far away to be a nebula. It had to be another galaxy outside the boundaries of our own.

Today, we know that there may be more than 50 billion galaxies. And many of these may contain hundreds of billions of stars. SEE ALSO BLACK HOLE; MILKY WAY GALAXY; PLANETARY SYSTEMS; STAR; UNIVERSE.

DEEP VIEW:
Seeing Into The Past

In October 1998 the Hubble Space Telescope trained its giant eye for 36 hours on an area just above the Big Dipper that looks almost empty to the naked eye. The Hubble's near-infrared camera took a long-time exposure and captured images (right) of the most far-away space objects ever seen—galaxies in formation as much as 12 billion or more years ago. The radiation from these galaxies has taken so long to reach us that we are actually seeing far into the distant past, long before the solar system and Earth even existed. The area of the sky in this picture is less than one hundredth as wide as the full Moon, yet it contains over 300 galaxies.

Galileo

Galileo Galilei (1564–1642) was an Italian astronomer. As a young university mathematics teacher, he taught that if two objects of different weights are dropped, they fall at the same speed. Other professors of the time taught that the speed of a fall was linked to the weight of an object.

After learning about the invention of the telescope by a Dutchman, Galileo built his own in 1609. Peering at the Moon, he saw craters and mountains. He observed that Venus went through phases like the Moon. He discovered four moons orbiting Jupiter, known today as the Galilean moons (Callisto, Europa, Ganymede, and Io).

Galileo believed that Earth and the other planets orbited the Sun. This was the idea of an earlier astronomer, Copernicus, and it went against the belief that the Sun and planets orbited Earth. Galileo's views angered other professors and the Roman Catholic Church. After disobeying orders to stop talking about his ideas, he was jailed for life inside his house. Galileo died in 1642, but his ideas lived on. Scientists such as Sir Isaac Newton used his work as the basis of their own and began to study the planets as a family of objects that orbit the Sun, not Earth. SEE ALSO NEWTON, SIR ISAAC.

Galileo demonstrated his telescope to the doge (ruler) of Venice, Italy, in 1609 on St. Mark's Square. Galileo built several telescopes after hearing of the "magic tube" invented by Hans Lippershey in Holland in 1608.

Ganymede

Ganymede is the largest of Jupiter's 16 moons and the largest moon in the solar system. It is one of the four moons Galileo discovered around Jupiter. Ganymede's diameter is 5,268 kilometers (3,270 miles), making it bigger than Mercury. Craters and grooves mark its surface.

Ganymede's oldest craters lie in its dark areas. One cratered area is about 3,200 kilometers (2,000 miles) wide. Newer craters dapple lighter areas.

Grooves like those on Ganymede don't exist on rocky planets such as Earth or Mars. Scientists believe the grooves formed when Ganymede was young. Heat inside the moon may have cracked the icy surface and water may have spilled out and froze. The icy crust may also have buckled as the moon cooled, creating more cracks, ridges, valleys, and plains.

Ganymede's icy crust covers a layer of water (blue) that may be ice or liquid. Below the layer of water is a rocky mantle (brown) surrounding a nickel-iron core (gray).

Ganymede is so large that if it orbited the Sun, it would be considered a planet. It seems to have a magnetic field around it, unlike any other moon. It also has a thin atmosphere of oxygen given off by its ice. SEE ALSO CALLISTO; EUROPA; IO; JUPITER; MOONS OF THE PLANETS.

Gas Giant Planets

A gas giant planet is made mostly of gases, but it contains liquid or even solid matter inside. In our solar system, the gas giant planets are Jupiter, Saturn, Uranus, and Neptune.

The atmospheres of the gas giants are thousands of miles deep. The weight of this deep atmosphere puts a lot of pressure on the lowest layers, creating heat and turning hydrogen from a gas into a liquid. Jupiter and Saturn have layers of liquid metallic hydrogen that conduct electricity. The two smaller gas giants, Uranus and Neptune, also contain liquid hydrogen but very little to none at all of the metallic variety.

Hydrogen and helium make up most of the atmosphere of gas giant planets. These two gases, hydrogen and helium, also make up stars. Each gas giant planet is thought to have a core of melted rock and ice. SEE ALSO JUPITER; NEPTUNE; SATURN; URANUS.

Glenn, John

John Glenn (1921–) was the first American astronaut to orbit Earth. Glenn was one of the Mercury 7, the seven astronauts picked to be part of the Project Mercury team. Project Mercury's goal was to learn more about sending humans into space.

On February 20, 1962, Glenn strapped himself into the one seat inside his space capsule, the *Friendship 7*. It sat on top of an Atlas rocket that towered 29.1 meters (95.3 feet) tall. At 9:47 A.M., the rocket blasted into space. A few minutes later, Glenn was in orbit around Earth.

Friendship 7 seemed to have a problem, however. An alarm indicated that its heat shield had come loose. Without a heat shield, the capsule would burn up when it reentered Earth's atmosphere. Flight controllers hoped that the straps holding a rocket onto *Friendship 7* would be strong enough to hold the shield in place. Luckily, the emergency turned out to be a false alarm caused by a faulty switch. Glenn splashed down safely in the Atlantic Ocean after orbiting Earth three times.

The journey lasted 4 hours and 55 minutes. During his flight, Glenn saw dazzling particles floating outside of his space capsule. Scientists figured out they were probably flecks of frost from the capsule, twinkling in the sunlight.

Glenn became a U.S. senator in 1974. On October 29, 1998, he blasted into space once again, this time aboard the space shuttle *Discovery*. The trip earned the 77-year-old Glenn the honor of being the oldest person to travel in space. SEE ALSO ASTRONAUTS AND COSMONAUTS; GAGARIN, YURI.

John Glenn was the first American to orbit Earth. On February 20, 1962, he sped around the globe in Friendship 7 at 28,000 kilometers (17,400 miles) per hour.

Goddard, Robert

Robert Goddard (1882–1945) was an American rocket engineer. Fascinated with rockets since boyhood, he was called the "moon rocket man."

Goddard was certain that rockets could fly in outer space—even though space lacks the oxygen needed for things to burn—by using liquid oxygen fuel. In 1919, he wrote about a rocket that could be flown to the Moon. Finally, on March 16, 1926, Goddard launched the first rocket to use liquid fuel. This rocket was powered by liquid oxygen and hydrogen.

Goddard's rockets were not the giant space vehicles we use today. His history-making first flight was launched from a cabbage patch in Worcester, Massachusetts, and flew only a few stories into the air. Later rockets he designed went as high as 2 kilometers (1.25 miles). Even so, Goddard's work made modern space flight possible. Liquid fuel powered the big Saturn V rockets that sent astronauts to the Moon and also powers the main engines of today's space shuttles. SEE ALSO VON BRAUN, WERNHER.

Gravity

Gravity is an invisible force that causes two objects to attract each other. Gravity weakens with distance. A more massive object has a greater force of attraction than a less massive one. This makes a less massive object move toward the more massive one.

If the lighter object (the less massive one) is moving fast enough and is at the right distance, it can escape falling into the heavier one. The Moon, for example, orbits Earth because of gravity. Earth's gravity attracts the Moon and keeps it from traveling in a straight line. But the Moon travels at the right speed and distance to keep it from falling straight into the Earth. Instead, it "falls" around Earth in a curved path. Likewise, gravity causes the other planets in our solar system to orbit the Sun. The orbiting space shuttle "falls" around Earth in the same way, following the curve of Earth's surface.

But if gravity is pulling on the shuttle, then why are shuttle astronauts weightless? Lack of gravity is not causing their weightlessness—even though astronauts call this condition "zero gravity." They are weightless because they are falling freely around Earth. They are said to be in "freefall." You would weigh nothing, too, if you were in freefall down a deep, deep hole into Earth's middle.

Gravity does more than keep objects in orbit. Jupiter's gravity, for example, is strong enough to capture objects such as comets and fling them into new orbits or cause them to crash into its atmosphere. Jupiter also twists the crust of its nearby moon Io, heating it up inside and causing volcanoes to erupt. Io is also tugged on by the gravity of the moons Ganymede and Europa! On Earth, ocean tides are caused mainly by the Moon's gravity.

On the Moon, gravity is only one-sixth as strong as on Earth because the Moon is much smaller than Earth. The pull of gravity is what gives you weight. If you weigh 100 pounds on Earth, you would weigh only 17 pounds on the Moon. This "weight loss" explains how astronauts can leap high on the Moon with little effort. On Jupiter, however, you would weigh 236 pounds.

Objects in space are not the only ones with gravity. All objects that have mass have gravity. An apple falling toward Earth, for example, is also pulling on Earth with its own tiny force of gravity. Earth is so much larger than the apple, though, that the apple's gravity has no apparent effect.

Scientists study how gravity behaves in the universe and what causes it. The space objects we know about do not add up to enough "stuff" to create all the gravity we see at work. Scientists think there is lots of "stuff," or mass, in the universe that we can't see. This hidden mass is called dark matter. Dark matter may make up 90 percent of the material in the universe. It may include black holes and bizarre particles much smaller than atoms, such as neutrinos. *SEE ALSO GALILEO; IO; JUPITER; NEWTON, SIR ISAAC; UNIVERSE.*

Greenhouse Effect

The greenhouse effect occurs when an atmosphere prevents heat from escaping the surface of a planet. Earth's atmosphere lets sunlight travel through it easily. This light warms the surface. The heat then returns to the atmosphere, where some is soaked up and continues to warm Earth like a cozy blanket. Some heat heads into space. Without the greenhouse effect, Earth would be a frozen planet.

On Venus, however, the greenhouse effect has turned the planet into a blast furnace with temperatures of 480°C (900°F). Venus became this hot because its thick atmosphere of carbon dioxide traps most of the heat given off by its surface. Astronomers think that Venus heated up long ago as the Sun boiled away its oceans and caused carbon dioxide to seep out of its rocks.

Some scientists warn that a runaway greenhouse effect may happen on Earth. It could be caused by the burning of fossil fuels, which adds carbon dioxide to the atmosphere. Cutting down forests might make the problem worse. Trees help soak up carbon dioxide, so preserving forests and conserving energy could help slow down global warming. *SEE ALSO ATMOSPHERE; EARTH; VENUS.*

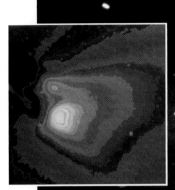

As Halley's comet passed through the solar system in 1910, the Royal Observatory in Cape of Good Hope, South Africa, took this beautiful picture. In 1986 when the comet visited again, the Giotto spacecraft got a close-up (upper left) of the comet's nucleus.

Halley's Comet

Halley's comet flies past Earth every 75 or 76 years as it makes one orbit around the Sun. It is named after Sir Edmond Halley, a British astronomer, who studied it and discovered some of the basic facts about comets.

Halley saw this comet in 1682. He observed that it traveled in the opposite direction of the planets—clockwise, not counterclockwise. He studied the paths of 24 other comets and discovered that comets travel in very elliptical orbits, unlike the planets.

Halley also figured out that two comets, which zoomed past Earth in 1531 and 1607, were actually the same comet that had passed by in 1682. He predicted that this comet would return again in 1758. Indeed it did, and it has returned three more times since then. In 1986, the last time Halley's comet approached the Sun, European and Japanese space probes greeted it. One of them, *Giotto*, got as close as 600 kilometers (375 miles) to the comet's head, or nucleus. This beautiful comet is a black lump of ice and dust measuring about 16 by 8 by 8 kilometers (10 by 5 by 5 miles). Its next visit will be in 2061. SEE ALSO COMETS; KUIPER BELT; OORT CLOUD.

Herschel, Sir William

Sir William Herschel (1738–1822) was an astronomer and music teacher who discovered the planet Uranus. In March 1781, Herschel was looking through one of his homemade telescopes, scanning the night sky as usual. This time, he spotted an odd dot of light in the constellation Gemini. It did not twinkle like a star. Herschel thought it might be a comet.

He kept an eye on it for the next few months. The round dot of light did not travel in a long elliptical orbit like a comet. Its orbit was nearly circular. Herschel had discovered a planet far beyond Saturn. In fact, it was twice as far from the Sun as Saturn. Herschel also discovered two moons of the planet.

Herschel suggested that the planet be named for the British king, King George III. French scientists called it Herschel. Finally it was named Uranus, after the Greek god who was the father of Saturn.

Herschel went on to direct the building of large telescopes. He continued studying the stars and also worked out how quickly the solar system was moving through space and in what direction. SEE ALSO MIMAS; URANUS.

Astronauts repair the Hubble Space Telescope (right) looming over the cargo bay of the space shuttle Endeavour. The telescope is named for the American astronomer Edwin Hubble (below).

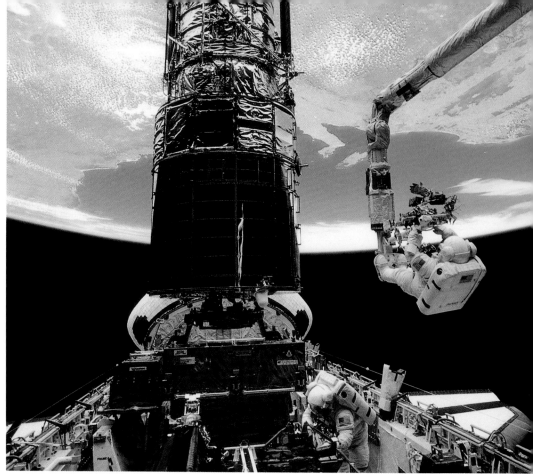

Hubble, Edwin

Edwin P. Hubble (1889–1953) was an American astronomer who proved in 1923 that other galaxies exist beyond our own Milky Way galaxy.

Hubble studied clouds of gas and dust called nebulae. In one of them, called the Andromeda Nebula, Hubble observed stars known as Cepheid variables. A Cepheid grows brighter and dimmer in a regular cycle. Over time every Cepheid with a cycle of a certain length gives off exactly as much light as any other Cepheid with a cycle of the same length, no matter how bright or faint it appears to us on Earth. Hubble's measurements of the Cepheids' light showed that the Andromeda Nebula was too far away to be in the Milky Way. It wasn't really a nebula at all but a galaxy we now call the Andromeda Galaxy.

Hubble sorted the galaxies into types: spiral, barred spiral, elliptical, and irregular. He discovered that most galaxies are speeding away from us, thus proving that the universe is expanding. He found that the farther away a galaxy is, the faster it's moving away from us. SEE ALSO GALAXY; MILKY WAY GALAXY.

Hubble Space Telescope

The Hubble Space Telescope is a telescope the size of a bus that orbits Earth. It holds a mirror 240 centimeters (96 inches) wide. This mirror collects light like an Earth-based reflecting mirror. But the Hubble is 596 kilometers (370 miles) above Earth. No atmosphere distorts its view of space. No city lights blot out the stars. Thus, the Hubble can see space objects that are difficult to detect from Earth.

The Hubble Telescope carries cameras and spectrographs—instruments that analyze the light given off by an object and tell scientists about its temperature, motion, and what it is made of. The Hubble can also detect near-infrared (heat) waves and ultraviolet light, which our eyes cannot see.

Since the Hubble was launched from the shuttle *Discovery* in April 1990, it has allowed scientists to peer into remote corners of the universe. Using the Hubble, scientists have viewed images of a star 100 times bigger than the Sun and clouds of gas and dust where new stars are being born. They have also studied images of 1,500 galaxies in a tiny patch of sky and detected clues indicating that black holes sit in the middle of some galaxies.

Closer to home, the Hubble photographed dust storms on Mars, volcanic eruptions on Jupiter's moon Io, and a comet colliding with Jupiter in 1994. It also peered at the asteroid Vesta, revealing that it may once have contained melted rock, like Earth does now.

The Hubble got off to a rough start, however. When it first went into orbit, the expensive telescope sent back blurry images. Scientists found out that the mirror's curve was incorrect. The mistake measured less than the width of a human hair—but it was enough to make the telescope much less useful. Scientists did a quick fix by writing new computer programs to sharpen the blurry images. Later, in 1993, astronauts aboard the shuttle *Endeavour* towed the Hubble into its bay. There they installed a set of mirrors that corrected the problem. The Hubble is expected to continue working through 2010. SEE ALSO TELESCOPES.

Io

Io is the solar system's hot spot. This moon of Jupiter seethes with volcanic activity. Less than one-third the diameter of Earth, it puts out twice as much heat. No other body in the solar system is more volcanically active. Because of this activity, no sign of Io's past exists. The lava and dust that have erupted from the volcanoes have erased all of Io's impact craters—those made by meteorites or asteroids. Today, the only craters on Io are volcanic ones. Many are huge. Io is dotted with at least 200 volcanic craters wider than 20 kilometers (12 miles).

In 1979, the spacecraft *Voyager 1* darted past Io. The pictures it took showed a pizza-colored world with up to nine volcanic eruptions taking place. Plumes of material reached hundreds of miles above the surface, shooting out of the volcanoes at speeds faster than any volcano on Earth.

The spacecraft *Galileo*, flying by Io in 1997 and 1998, found other amazing evidence of Io's volcanic activity. It showed that in just five months, the moon developed a huge dark spot as big across as the state of Arizona. The spot is an area 398 kilometers (249 miles) wide around a volcanic area called Pillan Patera. It seems to be made up of dark lava and a lighter gray fallout of dust from an eruption.

Studying these clues helps scientists figure out what kinds of materials make up Io and spew from its volcanoes. Io's red, yellow, orange, white, and black patches are made up of sulfur, which rains down on its surface from volcanic plumes. The gray ash tells scientists that some lava may contain bits of rocks called silicates—similar to volcanic rock on Earth. The high temperatures may be a clue that some of these rocks contain magnesium. This kind of volcanic activity may be very much like what happened on Earth, Venus, and Mars when they formed.

Io is fiery because it is only 421,600 kilometers (262,200 miles) from Jupiter. That's a little farther than the Moon is from Earth, but Jupiter could hold over 1,000 Earths. Its gravitational pull raises Io's surface by 66 meters (200 feet). Two other moons, Ganymede and Europa, pull on Io as well. This tug-of-war produces enough friction inside Io to keep its volcanoes stewing. SEE ALSO CALLISTO; EUROPA; GANYMEDE; JUPITER; MOONS OF THE SOLAR SYSTEM.

Two views of Io show this volcanically active moon of Jupiter fully illuminated by the Sun (right) and as a crescent (left). A volcano with a plume of blue smoke erupts on the outside edge of the crescent and is shown magnified in the inset (lower left).

The fifth planet from the Sun, Jupiter is the largest planet in our solar system. Immense bands of storm clouds swirl at the top of its atmosphere, which is mostly hydrogen and helium. The gas giant spins so fast that it bulges at its equator.

Jupiter

Jupiter is the giant of our solar system, bigger than any of the other planets. About 1,300 Earths could easily fit inside it. Yet Jupiter is light for its size, weighing only about as much as 381 Earths.

Jupiter is one of the gas giant planets (the other gas giants are Saturn, Neptune, and Uranus). It is made mainly of gases and liquid hydrogen, not solid rock like Earth, so you could never stand on its surface. Jupiter's atmosphere contains mostly hydrogen and helium, and layers of clouds swirl around the planet.

The chemical makeup of Jupiter is very similar to that of a star. Stars are also made mainly of hydrogen and helium, but Jupiter is much smaller than the Sun and other stars. Jupiter would have to be 80 times larger and 70 times heavier to burn like a star.

Storms rage continually on Jupiter, with lightning bolts thousands of times stronger than those on Earth. Winds faster than those of a hurricane whip the clouds, dragging them east and west. It is fitting that the planet is named after the king of the gods in Roman mythology—Jupiter, the lord of the skies, thunder, and lightning.

Wild weather creates Jupiter's most famous feature: the Great Red Spot. This spot is a storm in the planet's southern hemisphere that has lasted for over 300 years. Sometimes the spot grows large enough to span three Earths. At other times, it shrinks to the size of one Earth. The spot spins

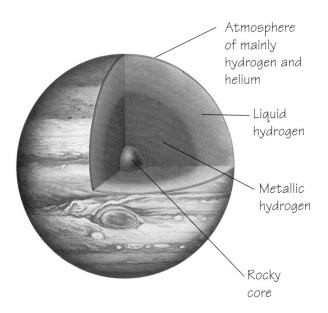

Atmosphere of mainly hydrogen and helium

Liquid hydrogen

Metallic hydrogen

Rocky core

The inside story: *Jupiter's atmosphere is made of hydrogen and helium. It surrounds a layer of liquid hydrogen. Beneath this lies another liquid layer of metallic hydrogen, which conducts electricity and may cause Jupiter's strong magnetic field. About 60,000 kilometers (37,000 miles) below the top of Jupiter's atmosphere lies a rocky core.*

JUPITER Fast Facts

Mass: 318 x Earth
Volume: 1,300 x Earth
Diameter at equator: 143,000 kilometers (88,800 miles). Largest planet
Distance from Sun: 779 million kilometers (484 million miles). Fifth planet from Sun
Moons: 16
Average temperature: -153°C (-243°F)
Time to rotate on axis at equator: 9 hours, 54 minutes
Time to orbit Sun: 11.9 years
Rings: Yes
Atmosphere: Hydrogen, helium

DID YOU KNOW?

Jupiter's thunderstorms are five times larger and more powerful than those on Earth. This computer-colored storm is 1,000 kilometers (620 miles) across.

completely around once every six days, making clouds ripple and winds roar. Our first images of this stormy atmosphere were beamed to us by *Pioneer 10*, which flew by Jupiter in 1973.

Although Jupiter is the biggest planet, it has the shortest day in the solar system. It spins completely around in a little less than 10 hours. The speed of the rotation causes this slushy planet to bulge out at the equator and flatten at the poles.

Jupiter's powerful gravitational pull keeps 16 moons orbiting it. Also in orbit around Jupiter is the unmanned space vehicle *Galileo*, which was launched in space by the shuttle *Atlantis* in 1989. After a journey of six years and 3.8 billion kilometers (2.4 billion miles), *Galileo* reached Jupiter in 1995. *Galileo* dropped a probe into the planet's atmosphere, which sent back information on chemicals and radiation in spite of furious winds that whipped it about. Then the probe melted and vaporized. *Galileo*, meanwhile, went on to orbit Jupiter.

In 1994, while *Galileo* was still on its way to Jupiter, it took photographs of Comet Shoemaker-Levy 9 smashing into the planet and transmitted the exciting images to scientists. *Galileo* has also sent back data on Jupiter's moons as part of its mission.

SEE ALSO CALLISTO; COMETS; EUROPA; GALILEO; GANYMEDE; GAS GIANT PLANETS; GRAVITY; IO; PLANETS OF THE SOLAR SYSTEM; VOYAGER MISSION.

Thin rings *of dust particles surround Jupiter. The dust is thrown from some of Jupiter's small moons when meteoroids crash into them. This color-enhanced image, taken by Voyager 2, looks back at the rings inside the planet's shadow.*

Kepler, Johannes

Johannes Kepler (1571–1630) was a German astronomer who discovered important facts about how planets move. Kepler believed in the theory of astronomer Nicolaus Copernicus, who stated that the planets orbit the Sun, not Earth, as most people then believed.

Like Copernicus, Kepler thought the planets' orbits were perfect circles. The problem with this idea was that the planets didn't behave properly. Seen from Earth, they seemed to move backward from time to time, then forward again. Kepler struggled to make the planets' motions fit in with the idea of round orbits but finally realized that the planets must have elliptical orbits.

Kepler discovered that planets move faster when they are close to the Sun and more slowly when they are farther away. He also showed that the distance between a planet and the Sun is related to the time it takes to orbit the Sun. SEE ALSO COPERNICUS, NICOLAUS.

Johannes Kepler's last book, which was published after his death, was about the possibility of life on the Moon.

Kuiper Belt

The Kuiper Belt is an area in the solar system that contains comets and other icy, rocky chunks. It is a storehouse of leftover bits from the solar system's formation 4.6 billion years ago. The Belt starts at the orbit of Neptune and reaches out to the beginning of the Oort Cloud beyond Pluto's orbit.

The Kuiper Belt rings the Sun much as the orbits of the planets do. It is a disk with the Sun at its middle. This makes it different from the Oort Cloud, which is like a round ball with the Sun at its center.

Scientists think comets that orbit the Sun every 200 years or less may come from the Kuiper Belt. Comets with longer cycles may come from the Oort Cloud. SEE ALSO COMETS; OORT CLOUD.

Life

Life on Earth includes plants, animals, fungi, and one-celled living things, such as bacteria and protozoa. All living things are made up of at least one cell and contain the element carbon. Chemical reactions inside cells release the energy that keeps living things alive and growing. Living things also reproduce themselves. So far, Earth is the only planet known to support life.

Earth formed about 4.6 billion years ago. The oldest rocks on Earth are about 3.8 billion years old. Fossils of single-celled organisms have been found inside rocks about 3.5 billion years old. Nearly 3 billion years went by before living things with more than one cell appeared. This was about 600 million years ago. Since then, many kinds of multi-celled plants and animals have come—and gone—on Earth.

Is there life elsewhere in the solar system? There does not seem to be any life on other planets. However, Mars continues to tantalize us because it once had water on its surface. Although no signs of life were found in Martian dirt when samples were tested in the 1970s, scientists did not give up their search. They are now studying meteorites from Mars. One meteorite is peppered with tiny pits that look as if they could have been made by bacteria. These bacteria would be smaller than any that exist on Earth.

Better places to look for signs of life, perhaps, may be the moons of the planets. One good candidate is Europa, which orbits Jupiter. It may have an ocean under its icy surface. Life on Earth developed in an ocean, so oceans are a good place to look.

Could life exist in places that are cold, with atmospheres full of methane, ammonia, and hydrogen? It might. Earth's early atmosphere was full of these chemicals. It was also very thin. It did not protect Earth from the Sun's radiation. Earth was also very warm and volcanic.

Even today, life on Earth exists in some very harsh places. There are worms that live in the ice of the Arctic and cannot survive in the warmth of your hand. Deep in the ocean, there are bacteria that live around hot vents. These hot-vent bacteria do not depend on sunlight for food as other life forms do. Instead, they make food from hydrogen sulfide, a chemical that flows from the vents. In turn, worms and other animals eat the bacteria.

Earth enjoys a good position in the solar system. It is just the right distance from the Sun so that it can have lots of liquid water. Water helps keep Earth's temperature from swinging wildly up and down between day and night.

Our atmosphere shields us from the harmful rays in the Sun's light. Life on Earth helped make this atmosphere. Early one-celled plants growing in the ocean 2 billion years ago gave off oxygen as a waste product. This oxygen began building up in the atmosphere, allowing other life forms to develop.

Scientists are also studying the universe for signs of intelligent life. Huge radio telescopes listen to the universe like giant ears, straining to catch a message from extra-terrestrial beings.

The biggest single-dish radio telescope is at the Arecibo Observatory in Puerto Rico. Its dish is the size of 26 football fields. Scientists from the SETI Institute use it to listen to radiation from space. (SETI stands for Search for Extra-Terrestrial Intelligence.) In the next few years, they will focus the telescope on one thousand stars that are like the Sun. They will watch closely for any signals that are different from the usual static from space.

In 1974, scientists sent a radio message from Arecibo to a cluster of far-off stars in the hope that some intelligent beings might intercept it. Nobody expects to get an answer very soon, though. It will take 21,000 years for our message to get there and the same amount of time for a reply to come back!

SEE ALSO EARTH; EUROPA; MARS; VIKING PROGRAM; WATER.

Lunar Eclipse

When Earth's shadow falls on the Moon and covers it completely, we see a lunar eclipse. Lunar means "of the moon." To eclipse means "to darken." A lunar eclipse happens when the Sun, Earth, and the Moon are lined up in a row, with Earth between the Sun and Moon. Then Earth's shadow (umbra) falls on the Moon. During a lunar eclipse, you can actually see Earth's shadow taking a bite out of the Moon's round shape.

We do not see a lunar eclipse very often. The Moon does not usually travel through Earth's shadow, because the Moon orbits Earth at a different angle compared to the Sun's path across our sky. Sometimes, only part of the Moon crosses Earth's shadow. This is called a partial lunar eclipse.

SEE ALSO MOON; SOLAR ECLIPSE.

During a lunar eclipse, the Moon often appears rusty red when it is totally in in shadow. Sunlight that has passed through the Earth's atmosphere makes the Moon's surface seem reddish.

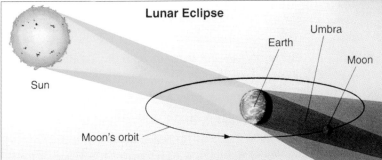

Lunar Eclipse

Sun

Earth

Umbra

Moon

Moon's orbit

The surface of Venus was revealed for the first time when the Magellan spacecraft (inset) sent back radar images of the planet in 1990.

Magellan Mission

Magellan was the first spacecraft to visit another planet after being launched from a space shuttle instead of an Earth-based launch pad. It left the shuttle *Atlantis* on May 4, 1989, and reached Venus on August 10, 1990.

Magellan used radar to map Venus's surface. The radar was able to see through Venus's thick clouds to the surface. *Magellan* also took pictures of volcanoes, craters, and other features. The information gathered by *Magellan* showed that the surface of Venus is not only very hot but very young. Lava from erupting volcanoes repaved much of the planet as little as 500 million years ago. SEE ALSO EXPLORATION OF THE SOLAR SYSTEM; MARINER SERIES; VENERA SERIES; VENUS.

Magnetic Fields

A magnetic field is the area around a magnet where the magnet's force is at work. Earth has a strong magnetic field, as if it contains a giant bar magnet connecting the planet's magnetic north and south poles. The ends of this magnet don't stay in one place, however. They may move a few miles back and forth in just one day!

A magnetic field can be produced by an electrical current. An electric wire, for example, has a magnetic field around it that will move a compass needle. In the same way, electricity in Earth's core produces a magnetic field around the planet. Earth's core has two parts—a solid inner core and a liquid outer core. Both parts contain iron. Liquid in the outer core swirls like a thick fluid being stirred. The motion of the liquid iron produces an electric current, which creates Earth's magnetic field.

Mars also has a magnetic field, but it is much weaker than Earth's. Scientists think that the liquid part of Mars's core flows too slowly to create much electricity. Or, it may be that the core of Mars is totally solid. A solid core can't move and produce electric currents or magnetism.

Like Mars, Mercury has a weak magnetic field. Scientists were surprised to find that it had any magnetic field at all. Mercury is so small that it was thought not to have a core. Several moons in the solar system cooled off so fast after forming that materials inside them did not have time to clump together and form layers. *Mariner 10*, however, discovered that Mercury has a large iron-nickel core that may be liquid enough to produce magnetism.

Venus is almost as big as Earth, but it rotates very, very slowly on its axis. So its magnetic field must come from someplace other than its core. Scientists think the Sun may create Venus's magnetic field. The Sun sends a stream of electrically charged particles, called ions, into space. This stream is called the solar wind. When the solar wind meets ions in Venus's atmosphere, magnetism is created.

The four big gas giant planets all have strong magnetic fields. Jupiter's is several thousand times stronger than Earth's! Both Jupiter and Saturn's magnetic fields are caused by electricity flowing in layers of liquid metallic hydrogen. Uranus and Neptune's fields may be caused by electrical currents in their liquid hydrogen layers. These two planets puzzle scientists, because if you imagined a bar magnet lying inside them, it would not be in the middle. It would lie off to one side.

A planet is totally surrounded by its magnetic field. Called a magnetosphere, the field is shaped like a teardrop on its side, with the round end facing the Sun.

A magnetosphere blocks most of the solar wind from hitting its planet. But bits of the solar wind still break through the magnetosphere. When they do, they create beautiful light shows called auroras. On August 27, 1998, a burst of magnetic activity on a star 20,000 light-years from Earth disturbed Earth's magnetic field. The star is believed to be a magnetar—a small, super-heavy star with a magnetic field a trillion times stronger than the Sun's. Its magnetic field is so strong that it caused a starquake, sending a blast of gamma rays into space. Some reached Earth and caused a light show in the sky. *See also Aurora; Planetary Cores; Solar Wind; Van Allen Belts.*

Mercury was photographed in 1974 by Mariner 10 (inset), which recorded about 45 percent of the surface. The pictures showed that Mercury is dotted with thousands of craters (right).

Mariner Series

The Mariner space probes studied Venus, Mars, and Mercury from 1962 to 1975. *Mariner 1*'s launch rocket failed in July 1962, but *Mariner 2* blasted off a month later and sailed off toward the Sun and Venus. The first spacecraft to visit another planet, *Mariner 2* sent back information on the Sun's magnetic field and Venus's very hot surface.

In 1965 *Mariner 4* was the first spacecraft to fly by Mars. It sent back photos of Mars and reported that the atmosphere is mainly carbon dioxide. *Mariner 9* was the first spacecraft to go into orbit around another planet. Launched in May 1971, it began orbiting Mars in November 1971 and photographed the planet's surface as well as its two moons.

Mariner 10 was the first and, so far, only spacecraft to fly by Mercury. It was launched in 1973 and reached Venus in 1974. Then it used Venus's gravity to get a boost on its journey to Mercury. It studied Mercury two more times after going into orbit around the Sun. In 1975, its job done, *Mariner 10* fell silent. *See also Exploration of the Solar System; Magellan Mission; Venera Series.*

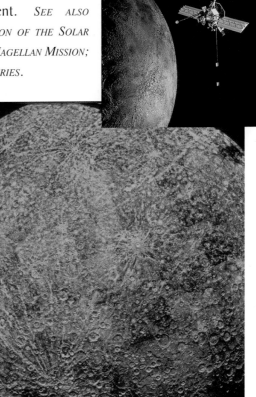

This magnificent view of Mars was pieced together from many different photos taken by Viking spacecrafts during the late 1970s. The giant canyon stretching across the center of the planet is Valley of the Mariners. It is between 2 and 7 kilometers (1.2 and 4.3 miles) deep and nearly as long as the United States is wide.

Mars

On July 4, 1997, a spacecraft slowed by a parachute and padded by air bags fell to the surface of Mars. It bounced and rolled for two minutes before coming to rest. Two days later, *Sojourner*, a six-wheeled vehicle the size of a microwave oven, rolled out.

Over the next 83 days, the little rover whirred around the Mars *Pathfinder* lander that had carried it into space. It sent over 550 images of Mars back to Earth. It analyzed the chemistry of rocks in its path, rocks that became known by such nicknames as Chimp, Yogi, Couch, and Barnacle Bill. On Earth, people followed *Sojourner's* travels as if it were an astronaut exploring Mars.

In some ways, Mars is like Earth. It has seasons, weather, clouds, and polar ice caps. Its axis tilts at a similar angle. A Martian day is 24 hours and 37 minutes long—just a bit longer than an Earth day. But there the similarities end. Mars, the fourth planet from the Sun, has a diameter only half as large as Earth's. It is much colder, and its gravity is only about a third as strong as Earth's. Mars has two tiny moons; Earth has one large one. Mars's atmosphere is 95 percent carbon dioxide and contains less than 0.2 percent oxygen. Earth's atmosphere is about 78 percent nitrogen and 21 percent oxygen.

With such a harsh environment, Mars is unlikely to be home to life as we know it. But the idea of life on Mars has long fascinated us. In past

The two-foot-long Sojourner is shown here before it rolled off its mothership, Pathfinder, after landing on Mars in July 1997. Beyond the white air bags is a boulder-strewn landscape. Many larger rocks were probably blasted from a nearby crater carved out when a meteorite crashed into Mars.

MARS Fast Facts

Mass: 0.1 x Earth
Volume: 0.15 x Earth
Diameter at equator: 6,794 kilometers (4,222 miles). Seventh largest planet
Distance from Sun: 227.9 million kilometers (141.6 million miles). Fourth planet from Sun
Moons: 2
Average temperature: -63°C (-81°F)
Time to rotate on axis: 24 hours, 37 minutes
Time to orbit Sun: 687 days
Rings: No
Atmosphere: Carbon dioxide

DID YOU KNOW?
The entire surface area of Mars is about equal to the land area of Earth.

centuries, people have wondered whether the dark patches on Mars were oceans or areas covered with plants. Others suggested that the channels on Mars were really canals built by intelligent beings.

In the 1960s, the United States sent Mariner spacecraft to Mars to view these and other mysteries of the Red Planet. They radioed back images of a planet with a thin atmosphere. In 1971, *Mariner 9* became the first spacecraft to orbit another planet. It sent back more than 7,000 images. In 1976, two Viking landers touched down on Mars. They photographed a rocky, red, desertlike land with a pinkish sky and sampled the dirt for signs of life.

Mars has a thin crust of rock colored red by abundant iron oxide. Beneath is a mantle of semi-molten rock. At the center is a core of molten iron.

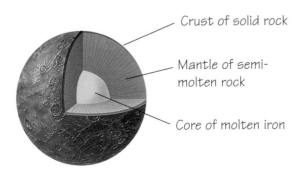

Crust of solid rock

Mantle of semi-molten rock

Core of molten iron

No life was found, but a photograph taken by a Viking orbiter showed a rock formation like a human face. Some people thought the face was part of an ancient Martian city. New photos taken by the *Mars Global Surveyor* showed that the "face" is nothing more than shadows cast by rock formations.

Even without life, Mars offers us much to wonder about. The size of its rocks and the way they are strewn about suggest that water may once have flooded Mars. Channels in the Martian surface hint at ancient rivers. Mars also boasts the solar system's tallest mountain and largest shield volcano (a volcano with wide, gentle slopes): Olympus Mons, rising 24 kilometers (15 miles) above a Martian plain. In addition, Mars has an enormous crater named Hellas about 2,100 kilometers (1,300 miles) wide. It is an impact basin—a crater created by something huge crashing into a planet or moon— and is perhaps the biggest such basin in our solar system.

Thirteen meteorites from Mars have been found on our planet. These bits of rock were knocked from Mars's surface a million or more years ago when a comet or asteroid hit it. Scientists have examined such meteorites closely for evidence of past life on Mars. *See also Life; Phobos and Deimos; Valley of the Mariners; Viking Series; Volcanoes; Water.*

The closest planet to the Sun, Mercury is so hot at its equator that lead would melt there. However, ice coats its poles, where the Sun barely gets above the horizon. There are no seasons on Mercury. Earth's seasons are caused by the way its axis tilts. Mercury's axis does not tilt at all. As the planet orbits the Sun, its axis remains perpendicular to the Sun.

Mercury

At first glance, Mercury seems a rather dull planet. No volcanoes erupt on its surface—they are all extinct. No storms whirl above it. No hints of possible life can be found. Mercury has barely any atmosphere and a very weak magnetic field. No moons orbit this small planet, which is not much bigger than Earth's Moon. A closer look at Mercury, however, reveals that it has had an exciting, violent history. Its craters, cliffs, and ice caps are the clues to discovering the planet's past.

Mercury is difficult to study from Earth because it is the closest planet to the Sun and often cannot be seen because the Sun's glow hides it. The spacecraft *Mariner 10* gave scientists their first close-up views of Mercury in 1974 and 1975. Photographs showed a planet dotted with craters, like Earth's

Moon, but with dark plains between the heavily cratered areas.

Mercury has a huge core of iron and nickel, which fills up nearly half the planet. This dense core gives Mercury a stronger gravity than the Moon has. When big objects smashed into Mercury and hollowed out craters, the planet's gravity prevented loosened rock from flying and falling far away from the points of impact. Instead, the rocks fell nearby, forming smaller craters close to the big ones. As a result, Mercury's surface alternates between areas densely pockmarked with craters and smooth plains. Mercury's volcanoes added to the plains by spreading sheets of lava across the planet's surface.

Lava played a part in creating Mercury's largest crater, the Caloris Basin. This basin is 1,300 kilometers (800 miles) wide. It formed when a huge object crashed into Mercury, splitting its surface. Lava welled up from the planet's interior and filled the basin, which cracked, buckled, and stretched under the lava's weight. Whatever hit the planet probably made it shake as a bell vibrates when its clapper strikes it. The shock waves from the crash traveled through the planet and shoved tall hills out of its other side.

Mercury also has long, steep cliffs as high as 3,200 meters (10,500 feet) or more. The longest

Crust of rock

Mantle of rock

Core of solid nickel and iron

Scientists believe Mercury has a thin crust of sun-baked rock covering a rocky mantle. A very large core of iron and nickel fills most of the planet and accounts for 70 percent of its diameter.

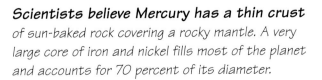

MERCURY Fast Facts

Mass: 0.06 x Earth
Volume: 0.06 x Earth
Diameter at equator: 4,878 kilometers (3,030 miles). Second smallest planet
Distance from Sun: 57.9 million kilometers (36 million miles). First planet from Sun
Moons: 0
Average temperature: 427°C (800°F) day; -183°C (-300°F) night
Time to rotate on axis: 59 days
Time to orbit Sun: 88 days
Rings: No
Atmosphere: None

DID YOU KNOW? Mercury is smaller than Saturn's largest moon Titan and Jupiter's largest moon Ganymede.

spans about 500 kilometers (300 miles). Scientists think these cliffs, called scarps, formed as the planet cooled down and shrank in size. The shrinking caused the surface to wrinkle, pushing up the cliffs.

Mercury's interior may have cooled off since the planet was created, but its surface bakes in the sunlight. Daytime temperatures on Mercury shoot up to 427°C (800°F). At night, the temperature plunges as low as −183°C (−300°F). The difference between Mercury's lowest and highest temperatures is 610°C (1,100°F)—the largest temperature range on a planet or moon. Despite the daytime heat, radar observations indicate that water ice exists in the shadowed craters of Mercury's north pole.

Mercury's temperature swings takes place in just one day, but a Mercury day lasts a long time. A day in the life of a planet equals the amount of time it takes the planet to spin around once on its axis. On Mercury, one spin takes 59 Earth days.

Mercury may dawdle through its day, but it zooms around the Sun faster than any other planet—in just 88 Earth days. This means Mercury orbits the Sun four times in just one Earth year. The speedy orbit explains why the planet was named after the ancient Roman god Mercury, the fleet-footed messenger of the heavens. SEE ALSO MARINER SERIES; PLANETS OF THE SOLAR SYSTEM.

Messier, Charles

Charles Messier (1730–1817) was a French astronomer who created a guide to objects in the sky and also discovered 19 comets.

Messier first became interested in astronomy as a boy of 14 when a great six-tailed comet appeared in the sky over his home in Lorraine.

When he was 21, Messier moved from Lorraine to Paris and studied under the official astronomer of the French navy, Joseph Nicolas Delisle. In 1757, Messier began looking for Halley's comet where Delisle had predicted it might appear. In 1758, he was thrilled to find a fuzzy object in the constellation Taurus but then noticed it never moved. It turned out to be a huge cloud of gas later named the Crab Nebula. Messier began listing objects that weren't stars so comet hunters would not make mistakes. He cataloged 103 objects. Later astronomers added seven more.

Each object is identified by a number and the letter M (for Messier). M1, for example, is the Crab Nebula. Today, astronomers still use Messier's numbers. SEE ALSO COMETS; GALAXY.

Meteoroids

Meteoroids are rocks and particles of dust that orbit the Sun. Some are bits and pieces left behind by comets. Others are chips off asteroids or chunks knocked out of the Moon or Mars.

Sometimes, meteoroids plunge into our atmosphere. Then they are called meteors, falling stars, or shooting stars. As the meteor rubs against air particles, it burns up, and the air it races through glows. The meteor burns up because this rubbing, or friction, produces heat. A meteor racing at 70 kilometers (45 miles) per second through the atmosphere sizzles at about 2,050°C (4,000°F). Most meteors burn up 80–120 kilometers (50–74 miles) above Earth.

When you see a meteor, it looks like a star streaking across the night sky. It may seem quite large, but it is really very small. Even a meteor as small as a pebble glows brightly. A big meteor that outshines the Moon is called a fireball. Some meteors explode high up in the atmosphere. Others actually hit the ground.

Meteors that strike Earth are called meteorites. Meteorites range in size from tiny dust particles to

Visible in broad daylight, *a big meteor passed over Grand Teton National Park in Wyoming on August 10, 1972. Scientists estimate that this object could have exploded with the force of a large nuclear bomb had it hit the ground rather than just skimming the atmosphere. Meteors usually cannot be seen in daylight. They are best seen at night during meteor showers, which occur when Earth passes through a cloud of dust left behind by a comet.*

the 45-meter-wide (150-feet-wide) meteorite that smashed into Earth about 49,000 years ago and left behind Barringer Meteor Crater in Arizona. This basin is 1,265 meters (4,150 feet) across.

Scientists estimate that several hundred tons of meteoroids enter Earth's atmosphere every day. Many of these are tiny dust motes too small to be noticed. Only the biggest ones reach Earth's surface. Scientists have found about 160 craters on Earth that were made by the largest of such impacts.

Most meteorites are black and are made of stone. They often lose their blackness after lying on the ground as wind and water affect them. A stony meteorite often has small rocks inside it. Some meteorites are stony-iron meteorites. They are half stone and half iron and nickel. Some are made almost completely of iron and a little nickel.

Most meteorites are also ancient rocks. They date back 4.6 billion years—to the time when the solar system was forming. Scientists value meteorites because they are like time capsules containing clues to the past. But younger meteorites are valuable, too. Meteorites that are only about 1.3 billion years old come from the Moon or Mars. So far, 13 Martian meteorites have been found on Earth.

One of these Martian meteorites, called ALH84001, was found in Antarctica. In 1996, scientists announced that it seemed to have fossils inside it. The fossils were tiny, hot-dog–shaped holes. Some scientists think that one-celled living things called bacteria made the holes. If this is true, they are half the size of the smallest bacteria ever found on Earth and would show that life once existed on Mars. So far, nobody has proved that the tiny holes and bumps are fossils—or that such incredibly small bacteria could have existed. See also Asteroids; Comets; Craters; Kuiper Belt; Life; Mars; Solar System.

Scientists disagree over whether the tiny worm-like shapes (inset) in the ALH84001 meteorite (below) are fossil bacteria from Mars.

ALH84001,0

The nearest major galaxy, the Andromeda galaxy, is over 2 million light years from our galaxy, the Milky Way. Astronomers believe this spiral galaxy looks much like ours, but it is almost twice as large.

Milky Way Galaxy

Our solar system of nine planets and one star is part of the Milky Way galaxy. A galaxy is a group of stars, gas, dust, and other matter held together by gravity. The Milky Way is one of billions of galaxies in the universe. Huge distances separate one galaxy from another.

The Milky Way galaxy is so big that light takes about 100,000 years to travel across it. Light travels faster than anything known—its speed is about 300,000 kilometers (186,000 miles) per second. A light-year is the distance that a beam of light travels in a vacuum in one year. Thus, we say that the Milky Way is 100,000 light-years wide.

If you could travel beyond the Milky Way, you would see that from the side it looks like a thin disk with a bulge in the middle. From above, it looks like a pinwheel with four or more arms spiraling out from its middle. Our solar system lies near one of those arms about halfway out from the galaxy's middle. The middle itself is a very large cluster of old stars. The rest of the Milky Way rotates around it. It takes our Sun about 240 million years to circle the middle of the Milky Way once.

Surrounding the galaxy is a giant "shell" of dark material that gives off little light. This shell holds much of the mass of the Milky Way. Its gravity pulls strongly on the stars in the Milky Way. Scientists are trying to identify this material.

Scientists estimate that the Milky Way contains 100 billion to 300 billion stars. Every star you see in the night sky is part of the Milky Way. From our point of view on Earth, its center sits in the constellation Sagittarius, though clouds of dust and gas block our view of it. On clear, moonless nights, you can sometimes see a patchy, glowing band spanning the sky. This band is the light from thousands of stars in our galaxy's spiral arms, which we are seeing from the side. SEE ALSO GALAXY; UNIVERSE.

Mimas

The little moon Mimas orbits Saturn just outside of the gas giant's ring system. It is only about 390 kilometers (240 miles) wide.

Mimas's biggest crater is 130 kilometers (80 miles) wide and 10 kilometers (6 miles) deep. Inside it a mountain rises 6 kilometers (19,685 feet) high—only about 600 feet less than Mt. McKinley, the tallest mountain in North America.

No other moon has a crater that is so large compared to its own size. Whatever hit Mimas and created this pit must have been huge—so big that scientists believe anything bigger would have smashed Mimas to bits.

Mimas's giant crater is named Herschel in honor of astronomer Sir William Herschel, who discovered Mimas. Astronomers nicknamed it "the Death Star " because its crater makes the moon look like the evil Death Star in the film *Star Wars*. SEE ALSO HERSCHEL, SIR WILLIAM; SATURN.

Miranda

Scientists did not expect to see anything exciting when *Voyager 2* flew past Uranus's moon Miranda in 1986. In fact, they were not even aiming for it. They were just sending the spacecraft past Uranus to get a boost from the planet's gravity. That boost would hurry *Voyager 2* on its way to Neptune.

As it turned out, the pictures *Voyager 2* sent back were amazing. Miranda was no ordinary icy, cratered chunk of rock. Instead, it was a mixture of grooves, mesas, cliffs, and wrinkles.

Miranda is only 470 kilometers (290 miles) wide. A giant V-shaped mark scars its middle. One canyon plunges 20 kilometers (12 miles) into the surface. A cliff called Verona Rupes reaches 15 kilometers (9 miles) high. Miranda also has high plains surrounded by stairlike cliffs.

Why does Miranda have all these odd landforms? One theory states that a huge object smashed Miranda to pieces not once but several times. Each time, gravity reunited the pieces, reforming the moon. Another theory holds that partially melted ices have welled up from time to time, creating Miranda's weird grooves, valleys, and cliffs. SEE ALSO MOONS OF THE PLANETS; URANUS.

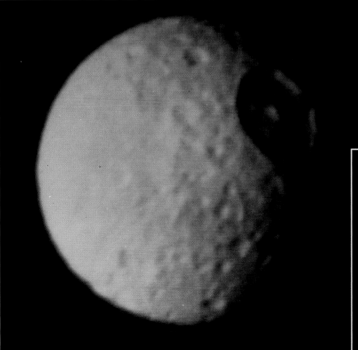

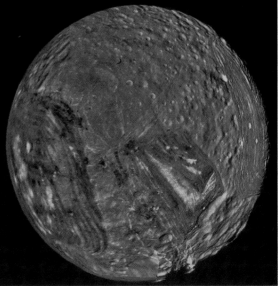

Called "the Death Star" *because of its huge crater, Saturn's moon Mimas (above) is about 390 kilometers (240 miles) wide. Uranus's oddly grooved moon Miranda (right) is only about 80 kilometers (50 miles) wider.*

A false-color image of the Moon (left) taken by the Galileo spacecraft shows the lava "seas" in dark blue and basaltic rocks in lighter blues and orange. Much of the surface is covered by a thin layer of fine rock powder visible in the Apollo 11 photo below.

Moon

At 10:56 P.M. Eastern Daylight Time on July 20, 1969, astronaut Neil Armstrong jumped down from the ladder of the lunar module *Eagle* and placed his boots in the Moon's powdery soil. For the first time, a human had set foot on a place in the solar system other than Earth. "That's one small step for a man," he said, "one giant leap for mankind."

Since taking that first small step, astronauts have landed on the Moon a total of six times. Moon rocks have been brought back for study. Instruments left on the Moon have measured moonquakes. Probes have photographed its surface. And in early 1998, the spacecraft *Lunar Prospector* orbited the Moon and found what seems to be ice in some craters. Scientists used to think there was no water on the Moon. Now it seems there may be lots of it!

The Moon is 385,000 kilometers (240,000 miles) from Earth. You could fit about 30 Earths between the two of them. If the Moon were much closer, Earth's gravity might pull it apart. Instead, Earth's gravity makes the Moon spin slowly so that the same side always faces Earth. The Moon's gravity affects Earth, too. It tugs on the planet and causes tides in the oceans. The Moon's gravity is not strong enough to hold onto an atmosphere.

If you lived on the Moon, you would weigh only one-sixth of what you weigh on Earth because there is less gravity on the Moon. (If you weigh 66 pounds on Earth, you would weigh only 11 pounds on the Moon.) You would need to bring air to breathe. You would also experience very long days. A Moon day lasts one Earth month because it takes the Moon about 27 Earth days to spin once on its axis. The Moon's orbit around Earth also takes about 27 days. This is why we always see the same side of the Moon facing us.

When humans are not visiting it, the Moon is a lifeless place. Scientists have found no evidence of life ever existing there. But they have found many clues to the Moon's history. The Moon is covered with craters left by asteroids and meteorites. There are no winds on the Moon to blow soil and erase

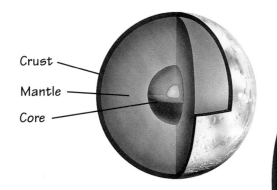

Crust
Mantle
Core

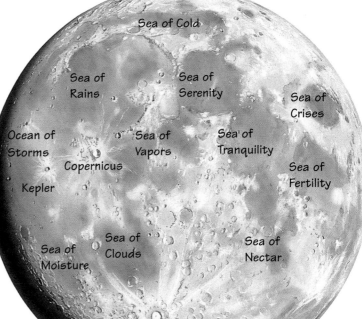

Sea of Cold
Sea of Rains
Sea of Serenity
Sea of Crises
Ocean of Storms
Sea of Vapors
Sea of Tranquility
Copernicus
Sea of Fertility
Kepler
Sea of Moisture
Sea of Clouds
Sea of Nectar
Tycho

Beneath the Moon's crust *is a mantle of rock partially molten near the core and a core of molten rock and metal. The Moon's many "seas" and craters (three are shown at right: Kepler, Copernicus, and Tycho) were made by meteorites crashing into the surface.*

craters, so very old ones still exist. Some are filled with hardened lava and look like "seas" or dark areas on the Moon. The Sea of Rains is a lava-filled crater 3.8 billion years old.

From Earth, the Moon seems to change shape. The changes are called the phases of the Moon. The phases occur because we see the Moon from different angles as it orbits Earth, and we can't always see all of the part of the Moon being lit by the Sun.

For example, we can't see the sunlit side of the Moon at all when the Moon is between the Sun and Earth. The side of the Moon facing us is, at this time, dark. We then see a bit more of the Moon each night over the next two weeks as it orbits Earth. We see the silvery full Moon when Earth is between the Moon and the Sun. Then the Moon seems to shrink over the next two weeks, and the cycle starts again.

Sometimes, the Moon and Earth line up in such a way that they block out the light of the Sun shining on each other. When the Moon blocks sunlight from the Earth, it is called a solar eclipse. When the Earth stops sunlight from reaching the Moon, it is called a lunar eclipse.

The Moon is about a quarter of Earth's diameter, making it a large moon compared to its planet. How did Earth and the Moon team up? Scientists think that the Moon formed from material blasted out of the newly formed Earth when it was hit by a big object. *SEE ALSO EARTH; MOONS OF THE PLANETS.*

MOON Fast Facts

Mass: *0.01 x Earth*
Volume: *0.02 x Earth*
Diameter at equator: *3,476 kilometers (2,160 miles)*
Distance from Earth: *385,000 kilometers (240,000 miles)*
Average temperature: *107°C (224°F) day; -153°C (-243°F) night*
Time to rotate on axis: *27.32 days*
Time to orbit Earth: *27.32 days*
Atmosphere: *None*

DID YOU KNOW?
Scientists think that there may be millions of tons of water in the form of frost and ice buried beneath the surface of the Moon's polar regions.

The Moon's South Pole

Six of Saturn's 18 known moons are visible in this collage of images. All were photographed by the Voyager 1 spacecraft during its close encounter with Saturn in November 1980. Dione is shown large, in front, with Saturn rising behind it. Tethys and Mimas are to the left of Dione. Enceladus and Rhea are directly above Dione. Saturn's largest moon, Titan, is in the upper left-hand corner of the picture.

Moons of the Planets

A moon is a natural object that orbits a planet or an asteroid instead of the Sun. Earth's Moon is its only moon. Other planets have more. Saturn has 18 known moons (and possibly two more). Uranus also has 18 moons. The eighteenth moon was discovered in 1999. Mercury and Venus have no moons.

The many moons of our solar system come in a variety of shapes and sizes. Earth's Moon is a round ball. Hyperion, a small moon orbiting Saturn, looks more like a hamburger. The tiny moons of Mars look like potatoes. One of these moons, Deimos, is among the smallest known moons in the solar system. It is only about 11 kilometers (7 miles) wide. A car driving at highway speeds could travel completely around it in about eight minutes. The largest moon is Ganymede, which orbits the biggest planet, Jupiter. Ganymede is twice as massive as

Earth's Moon and bigger than Mercury and Pluto.

Earth's Moon is airless and lifeless. So, too, are the moons of Mars. Scientists are studying the moons of the four gas giant planets (Jupiter, Saturn, Uranus, and Neptune) for signs of life. *Voyager 2* swept past the gas giant planets on a grand tour from 1979 to 1989. It discovered three new moons around Jupiter, three new moons around Saturn, 10 new moons around Uranus, and six new moons around Neptune.

MOONS Sixty-four and No Two Alike

Planet	Number of Moons	Interesting Facts
Earth	1	The spacecraft *Lunar Prospector* discovered that the Moon has lots of water ice at its poles and a small core at its center.
Mars	2	One moon, Deimos, is one of the smallest in the solar system; the other, Phobos, will someday crash into Mars.
Jupiter	16	Jupiter's moon Ganymede, the largest moon in the solar system, is surrounded by dust caused by meteorites hitting its surface.
Saturn	18	Saturn's moon Titan, second largest moon in the solar system, has a thick atmosphere filled with orange clouds.
Uranus	18	The spacecraft *Voyager 2* discovered 10 moons when it visited Uranus in 1986.
Neptune	8	Neptune's moon Triton orbits its planet in a clockwise direction, unlike other big moons in the solar system.
Pluto	1	Pluto's moon, Charon, is half as big as Pluto but wasn't discovered until 1978.

Europa, one of the Jovian moons (moons of Jupiter), is covered with ice. Beneath the ice, there may be an ocean. The same may be true of Callisto, the most crater-pocked moon in the solar system. If these Jovian moons have oceans, they will be the only other liquid oceans known to exist in the solar system. Such oceans might even hold life.

Another intriguing moon is Io, which also orbits Jupiter. Io has the most volcanic activity of any place in the solar system. Titan, a moon orbiting Saturn that is bigger than Mercury, is the only moon known to have a thick atmosphere. Saturn's moon Enceladus is covered with white ice and reflects more light than any other moon or planet. Some of Saturn's moons share orbits. Another of Saturn's moons, Iapetus, is black on one side and white on the other.

How did the planets come to have moons? Some moons orbiting the gas giant planets may have formed at the same time as the planets. Material that didn't clump together to form a planet may have formed smaller bodies instead. The gravity of the gas giant planets was strong enough to attract these small bodies and keep them in orbit.

Some moons may have been born in other ways. Scientists think our Moon formed from material knocked out of the early Earth when a large object hit it. The moons of Mars may be asteroids trapped by Mars's gravity. Some of Jupiter's smallest moons may be pieces left over after collisions. Phoebe, Saturn's most distant moon, may be a comet captured by Saturn's gravity. Miranda, one of Uranus's moons, is heavily scarred. Some scientists think it may have once shattered to bits, then glued itself back together again.

A planet's gravity keeps a moon from drifting into space. It also may make the moon's rotation slow down until the moon's day takes as long as one orbit around the planet. A moon's gravity can affect its planet, too. The gravitational force of Earth's Moon, for example, causes high and low tides in the oceans. It also slows Earth's rota-tion by two-thousandths of a second every 100 years. *SEE ALSO CALLISTO; CHARON; GANYMEDE; IO; MIMAS; MIRANDA; PHOBOS AND DEIMOS; TITAN; TRITON.*

NASA

NASA stands for the National Aeronautics and Space Administration. It is a government agency whose mission is to study the atmosphere, space, and ways to use space.

NASA's headquarters are in Washington, D.C., but it also operates sites all over the United States. For example, NASA launches shuttles from the Kennedy Space Center in Florida. It trains astronauts and controls space missions at the Johnson Space Center in Texas. It designs satellites at the Goddard Space Flight Center in Maryland and rockets at the Marshall Space Flight Center in Alabama. It plans missions by robot spacecraft to other planets at the Jet Propulsion Laboratory in California. California is also home to the Ames Research Center. Space telescopes and probes sent into deep space are developed there. *SEE ALSO CAPE CANAVERAL; EXPLORATION OF THE SOLAR SYSTEM.*

The Jet Propulsion Laboratory, run for NASA by the California Institute of Technology, plans flights of unmanned spacecraft to other planets at its headquarters (below) in Pasadena, California.

Neptune

Neptune is a blue-green planet about 1.6 billion kilometers (1 billion miles) beyond Uranus. It is about the same size as Uranus—its diameter is 49,532 kilometers (30,775 miles), only 1,590 kilometers (990 miles) less than its "twin" Uranus.

Both Neptune and Uranus are stormy places, with winds reaching up to 1,320 kilometers (818 miles) per hour. Even though Neptune is so much farther from the Sun than Uranus, its frigid atmosphere is about the same temperature as the atmosphere of Uranus. Neptune's heat comes from the energy inside the planet.

The fourth largest planet in the solar system, Neptune is also the smallest of the four gas giant planets (the other gas giants are Jupiter, Saturn, and Uranus). Neptune most likely contains a slushy, rocky, icy core wrapped in a layer of liquid hydrogen. Its atmosphere, like that of the other gas giants, is made up largely of hydrogen, helium, and

This painting shows Neptune (left) as it might look from its largest moon, Triton. A liquid methane geyser shoots up from blue-and-pink nitrogen and methane ices on Triton's surface. The distant Sun can be seen just to the right of the geyser's top.

methane. Bright white clouds drift across its face. One large cloud named Scooter was observed zipping around the planet's southern hemisphere.

Swirling clouds and high winds created a Great Dark Spot on Neptune much like Jupiter's famous Great Red Spot. This Earth-sized spot was recorded by *Voyager 2* when it flew past Neptune in 1989. By 1994, though, photographs from the Hubble Space Telescope showed that the Great Dark Spot had completely disappeared.

Neptune remained a secret for nearly 65 years after the discovery of Uranus in 1781. It was a wobble in Uranus's orbit that led astronomers to Neptune.

For more than 200 years, scientists have been able to predict where and when a planet, comet, or other known solar system object will appear. Using math, they calculate the object's size, speed, and the path of its orbit. But scientists in the late 1700s and early 1800s noticed that the planet Uranus wasn't following the rules; it did not always appear where it should. Some gravitational force was tugging on Uranus and affecting its orbit.

In 1845 and 1846, two astronomers working separately figured out how big that "something" was and where it would be. One of them, Urbain Le Verrier, sent his work to a German astronomer, who then spotted Neptune through his telescope exactly where Le Verrier had said "something" would be. Some astronomers believed that Neptune also had a wobble in its orbit—which led them to search for yet another new planet!

Neptune's path around the Sun crosses Pluto's orbit. As a result, Neptune sometimes becomes the farthest planet from the Sun. Neptune became the outermost planet in 1979, but in 1999 Pluto once again moved beyond Neptune and will remain the farthest planet until 2231.

A series of five rings orbit Neptune. The rings are made of black matter that does not reflect light, just like the matter in the rings of Uranus. Most of this matter consists of tiny dust particles, but some chunks are about the size of a school bus.

Eight moons orbit Neptune. The largest of them, Triton, circles Neptune in a clockwise direction while Neptune spins counterclockwise. No other big moon in the solar system orbits backward like this. Triton is also the coldest place that has yet been measured in the solar system, with temperatures that plunge as low as −234°C (−389°F).

Just past Neptune lies the Kuiper Belt, an area stretching from Neptune to beyond Pluto that holds comets, ice, and other material. Neptune's gravity sometimes snatches comets out of the Kuiper Belt and slings them toward Jupiter. Neptune may even have trapped some of its moons. Triton may once have orbited the Sun on its own before being caught by Neptune's gravity. *SEE ALSO GAS GIANT PLANETS; GRAVITY; HERSCHEL, SIR WILLIAM; KUIPER BELT; PLANETARY CORES; PLANETS OF THE SOLAR SYSTEM; PLUTO; TRITON.*

NEPTUNE Fast Facts

Mass: 17 x Earth
Volume: 58 x Earth
Diameter at equator: 49,532 kilometers (30,775 miles). Fourth largest planet
Distance from Sun: 4,498 billion kilometers (2,793 billion miles). Eighth planet from Sun
Moons: 8
Average temperature: -215°C (-356°F)
Time to rotate on axis: 16 hours, 7 minutes
Time to orbit Sun: 165 years
Rings: 5
Atmosphere: Hydrogen, helium, methane

DID YOU KNOW?

Except for some white clouds of ammonia crystals, Neptune is blue because its atmospheric methane absorbs all the colors of sunlight but blue.

Neptune's frigid atmosphere *generates some of the solar system's stormiest weather. When Voyager 2 took this picture in 1989, the Great Dark Spot (a storm as large as Earth) was whipping up giant white clouds of ammonia crystals. Five years later, the spot had vanished.*

Newton, Sir Isaac

Sir Isaac Newton (1643–1727) was one of the greatest scientists of all time. His experiments and ideas completely changed the study of science. Many of his discoveries still stand as laws of physics today.

Newton, an Englishman, is most famous for his work on gravity. A popular story tells how Newton discovered gravity when he saw an apple fall from a tree. This tale may or may not be true. However, Newton was the first to describe how gravity worked. He explained how the same force that makes an apple fall to the ground also makes the Moon orbit Earth.

Other scientists had tried to explain why the Moon orbited Earth and how planets orbited the Sun. Some of these ideas involved magic. Others pointed to magnetism or whirlpools in space. But

Sir Isaac Newton *used prisms to demonstrate his theory that although sunlight appears white, it is actually a blend of various different colors.*

Newton showed that the invisible force of gravity is what holds the universe together and makes it work. He came up with a mathematical formula that shows how gravity pulls less strongly on objects as the distance between them increases.

Newton wrote about gravity in a book called, in short, *Principia.* He also wrote about laws of motion in this book—laws that explain how and why objects move, speed up, slow down, and attract each other.

Newton made important discoveries about light. He used prisms to show that sunlight, or white light, is made up of light of different colors. Other people had seen prisms make little rainbows before. But they thought this happened because prisms varied in thickness, producing lighter or darker colors depending upon where light passed through them.

Newton's work with light led to his invention of the reflecting telescope, the type used in most observatories today. Math students around the world also work with another of Newton's inventions, a branch of mathematics called calculus. *SEE ALSO GRAVITY; ORBIT; SPECTRUM.*

North Star (Polaris)

The North Star (also called Polaris) isn't the brightest or biggest star in the night sky of the northern hemisphere. But it is the only one that stays in one place from our point of view. The northern end of Earth's axis points almost straight at Polaris. (The axis is an imaginary line through the middle of Earth around which the planet spins.) All the other stars appear to circle around Polaris in a 24-hour cycle.

Polaris is like a signpost in the sky that signals "This way is north." It has guided many explorers on their journeys. You can always find Polaris if you can find the group of stars called the Big Dipper. The two stars on the side of the Dipper opposite the handle always point to Polaris regardless of whether the Dipper is beneath or above Polaris.

Polaris, however, has not always been the North Star. About 5,000 years ago, the star Thuban was the North Star. In 5,000 years, a star called Alpha

A gigantic cosmic junk yard, the Oort Cloud is a globe-like swarm of perhaps a trillion or more comets orbiting the Sun far beyond Pluto, the outermost planet. A comet from the Oort Cloud may have caused the extinction of the dinosaurs 65 million years ago.

Cephei will become our North Star. This change occurs because Earth wobbles as it spins. Over time, its axis travels in a circle and points to different places in the sky. SEE ALSO CONSTELLATIONS.

Oort Cloud

The Oort Cloud is an area of space containing matter left over from the formation of the solar system. It surrounds the solar system the way the white of an egg surrounds the yellow yolk. The Oort Cloud starts way beyond Pluto's orbit and reaches about one-sixteenth of the way to Proxima Centauri, the closest star to our solar system.

The Oort Cloud is believed to contain over a trillion "sleeping" comets. Occasionally, a comet is pushed out of the Oort Cloud and begins to orbit

the Sun. This push may take place when two comets collide or when a large object, such as Neptune, pulls a comet out with its strong gravity.

Not all comets come from the Oort Cloud. Some may come from the Kuiper Belt, an area that stretches from Neptune to beyond Pluto. Scientists think that comets that take thousands of years to complete one orbit around the Sun come from the Oort Cloud. So, too, do comets that travel paths tipped at an angle to the orbits of the planets.

The Oort Cloud is named after astronomer Jan Hendrick Oort, who in 1950 theorized that this cloud existed. Earlier, in 1927, Oort discovered that the Milky Way rotates around its center. He also showed that our solar system lies nearer the galaxy's edge than its middle and that the galaxy is spiral shaped. SEE ALSO COMETS; KUIPER BELT; SOLAR SYSTEM.

O-P

Orbit

An orbit is the path a space object travels as it goes around another space object. Moons, for example, orbit planets. Earth and the other planets orbit the Sun. The solar system orbits around the center of our galaxy. Moons and planets orbit in paths called ellipses that are nearly circular. Comets and asteroids have long, squashed elliptical orbits.

Moons orbit planets because the planets' gravitational pull stops them from sailing off into space and makes them travel in a curved path instead. Likewise, the Sun's gravitational pull holds the planets in orbit around it. The planets avoid being sucked into the Sun by moving at high speed. The closer a planet is to the Sun, the faster it orbits.

Space shuttles and man-made satellites orbit Earth. They are really "falling" nonstop around Earth. At such heights, there is little air and therefore not much friction, or rubbing against air, to slow a spacecraft—but there is just enough drag so that gravity slowly tugs it back to Earth. If a shuttle falls below its proper orbit, astronauts fire rockets to boost it up to its correct orbit.

Can a moon fall into its planet? It can—but only if it moves too close to the planet. Such a moon can be tugged into closer and closer orbits. At a certain point, it explodes or crashes into the planet. Scientists think that the moon Phobos will smash into Mars millions of years from now. (Our Moon, however, is not on a crash course with Earth.)

Gravity not only keeps objects in orbit, but can also change orbits. Jupiter's strong gravity can pull rocks out of the asteroid belt and comets out of the solar system. Neptune's gravity can pull comets from the edges of the solar system and toss them into new orbits. The big planets may also have caught objects with their gravity and trapped them in orbits, turning them into moons.

About 400 years ago, people thought the Sun, planets, and stars orbited Earth. Copernicus, Kepler, and Galileo proved that Earth and other planets orbited the Sun. SEE ALSO COPERNICUS, NICOLAUS; GALILEO; GRAVITY; KEPLER, JOHANNES.

Phobos and Deimos

In 1971, a huge dust storm swirled across Mars just as the spacecraft *Mariner 9* was zooming in for a look at the Red Planet. So scientists detoured the craft past Mars's two small moons, Phobos and Deimos. They turned out to be strange objects indeed. Neither is round. Both are very dark.

Phobos is an oval lump of rock pitted with craters, only about 26 kilometers (16 miles) long. It is covered with about 260 craters. The biggest is called Stickney Crater. It is 10 kilometers (6 miles) across, almost half as wide as the moon itself. Scientists think Stickney formed after a crash that nearly broke Phobos into pieces.

Even smaller than Phobos, Deimos is only 12 kilometers (7 miles) across. *Viking 2* flew within just 24 kilometers (15 miles) of Deimos in 1977. Its cameras showed that Deimos was smoother than Phobos. Many of its craters are covered by dust.

The two moons orbit Mars in very different ways. Phobos is closer to Mars. It orbits at a distance of only 9,400 kilometers (5,800 miles) and

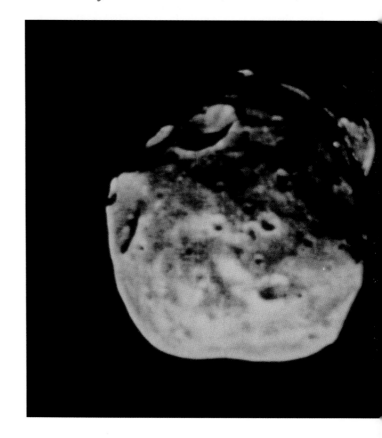

whips around Mars in just seven hours. It is moving closer to Mars every year. Scientists think it will crash into Mars in 40 to 70 million years.

Deimos, on the other hand, is 23,500 kilometers (14,600 miles) from Mars. It orbits Mars in about 30 hours—a bit longer than one Martian day.

If you were to visit Phobos, you might find walking difficult because its surface is hip-deep in powdery dust. Scientists figured this out by looking at images sent back in 1998 by the Mars *Global Surveyor*, which began orbiting Mars in 1997. Phobos's dust has been blasted out of its surface by meteoroids over millions of years. Phobos's gravity would not slow you down, however. It is only one one-thousandth of Earth's gravity, just enough to hang on to its dust and rocks. If you were standing on Phobos, you could throw a baseball into orbit.

These odd moons may be asteroids captured by Mars's gravity. Phobos and Deimos are the names of two sons of Mars, the Roman god of war. *SEE ALSO ASTEROIDS; GRAVITY; MARS; MOONS OF THE PLANETS.*

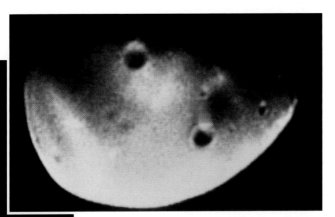

Phobos and Deimos, *Mars's tiny moons, were probably once asteroids from the far edge of the asteroid belt. Jupiter may have pulled them out of their original orbits around the Sun and sent them hurtling toward Mars, where they were captured by the Red Planet's gravity. This false-color image of Phobos (left), the larger of the two moons, shows that it has many craters. The false-color image of Deimos (above) reveals a smoother surface with fewer craters.*

Pioneer Program

The Pioneer Program consisted of a series of space missions that started in 1958. The most famous Pioneer spacecraft are *Pioneer 10* and *11*.

Pioneer 10 was launched in March 1972. It achieved a lot of space "firsts." It was the first spacecraft to fly beyond the orbit of Mars, the first to travel through the asteroid belt, and the first to take close-up pictures of Jupiter. It also mapped Jupiter's magnetic field and discovered that it is bigger than the Sun with a teardrop tail that stretches all the way to Saturn's orbit. On June 13, 1983, *Pioneer 10* became the first spacecraft to go beyond our solar system. *Pioneer 11* traveled hot on *10's* heels. It was launched in April 1973 and followed the same path as *Pioneer 10* to Jupiter. Then it got a boost from Jupiter's gravity and zoomed toward Saturn. There, *Pioneer 11* found new rings.

Now both *Pioneer 10* and *11* are drifting nearly 11.3 billion kilometers (7 billion miles) from the Sun. *Pioneer 10* is set to examine the "heliopause"—the place where gases from the Sun meet interstellar space. It takes over 18 hours for *Pioneer 10's* messages to reach Earth. When the battery power of the spacecraft dies, it will be out of our reach forever. Both Pioneers carry messages etched in metal on them. The messages are for any intelligent alien beings that may one day find the spacecraft. The messages may help these beings figure out where the spacecraft came from—and that they come in peace.

What happened to the first nine Pioneers? *Pioneers 1, 2,* and *3* were launched to go to the Moon but never made it. The first didn't go fast enough to escape Earth's gravity. The second and third didn't launch properly. *Pioneer 4* flew past the Moon but was too far away to gather information. *Pioneer 5* to *9* were launched into orbit around the Sun. Two later Pioneer spacecrafts, *Pioneer-Venus Orbiter* and *Venus Multiprobe*, were launched in 1978. The *Orbiter* mapped most of Venus's surface. The *Multiprobe* dropped probes into Venus's atmosphere. *SEE ALSO EXPLORATION OF THE SOLAR SYSTEM.*

A *modern planetarium* uses computer-controlled projectors and often laser lights to imitate the night sky. The projectors can show not only heavenly objects but also other things such as lines indicating the coordinates of stars and planets.

Earth. The projector can also move and show the sky in motion. It can be programmed to show the stars moving across the sky and how the planets move against this starry background and to show other space objects such as comets and meteoroids. *SEE ALSO CONSTELLATIONS; PLANETS OF THE SOLAR SYSTEM.*

Planetary Cores

A planetary core is the material in the center of a planet. Wrapped around the core is a layer called the mantle. The mantle may have layers within it, too. On top of the mantle is the surface, or crust. Above this is the atmosphere.

Planetary cores are as different as the planets themselves. Earth's core, for example, is a ball of solid iron and nickel surrounded by liquid iron and nickel. The solid part is called the inner core. The liquid part is called the outer core. The inner core is incredibly hot but does not melt because it is under great pressure. Here, the weight of the layers above press down with a force over 3 million times stronger than the air pressure you feel on Earth's surface. The outer core is under less pressure, so it stays liquid at 4,100°C (7,400°F). Scientists think that Earth's magnetic field is created by the flow and motion of the liquid outer core.

Earth is a rocky planet. Jupiter, on the other hand, is a gas planet. Much of it is made up of liquid hydrogen. The great pressure of the atmosphere above it keeps this liquid from becoming a gas. If Jupiter has a solid surface, we have not found it yet. However, scientists think Jupiter has a very dense core. It is probably a ball of melted rock. Jupiter's core may hold enough material to give it the weight of 20 Earths.

Planetary cores are difficult to study. We can't travel to Earth's center even though it is only 6,400

Planetarium

A planetarium is a building that uses a special projector and screen for showing scenes of the night sky. The ceiling is dome-shaped. The screen covers the inside of this dome. People sit beneath the dome in the dark and watch stars, planets, and the Moon as they are projected on the screen.

The projector is specially designed to shine light onto the screen in the same pattern as the stars in the night sky. It can show how the sky looks at any time of the day, month, or year from any spot on kilometers (4,000 miles) beneath our feet. Pressure and temperature increase as one drills deeper into Earth. There is no way to survive such a crushing, scorching journey—even if we had the tools to take us there. So how do scientists find out about Earth's core and what is inside of distant planets?

On Earth, scientists study earthquakes. They measure how an earthquake's vibrations travel through Earth. The vibrations behave in different ways as they travel through different materials. By examining these changes, scientists can discover what the different materials are.

Space probes and telescopes help us find out about other planets. Scientists watch planets and measure their movements—how they rotate, how they orbit, and how the planets make other space objects behave. They also analyze information gathered by space probes.

We know, for example, that Jupiter is very hot inside because temperatures go up as pressure goes up—and the pressure is very great inside such a big planet. Another clue is that Jupiter gives off about twice as much heat as it gets from the Sun. We also know that Jupiter's gravity is very strong by watching how the planet affects moons and other objects near it. Using this information, scientists have estimated the thickness of various layers in Jupiter.

Scientists also study the light reflected by far-off planets to figure out what materials are in them.

Space probes help us find out what kinds of chemicals, ices, and rocks form a far-off space object, too. If we know what the materials are, then we know a lot about how they behave when they are heated, cooled, or put under pressure.

Space probes can also measure a planet's magnetic field to find out what's inside. The strength of the magnetic field is a clue. A planet with a strong magnetic field probably has a liquid metallic layer.

In this way, scientists have figured out that Saturn, Uranus, and Neptune probably have rocky cores like Jupiter's. Tiny Mercury has a huge iron core that forms 44 percent of the volume of the planet. Scientists think much of its outer layer was blasted away by a crash long ago. Venus and Mars both have cores of iron and nickel, and Pluto has a rocky core.

How did planets form cores? We don't know for sure, but the planets probably formed from clouds of dust and ice circling the Sun over 4 billion years ago. Gravity made the dust and ice clump together.

There are two ways this clumping might have happened. The heaviest materials, such as rock and iron, may have clumped first. Then lighter materials collected around this core of heavy materials. Or, all materials may have clumped together to form a ball, no matter how heavy they were. Then the heavy materials in the ball sank into the middle while the lighter ones floated upward. *SEE ALSO GAS GIANT PLANETS; GRAVITY; SOLAR NEBULA; TERRESTRIAL PLANETS.*

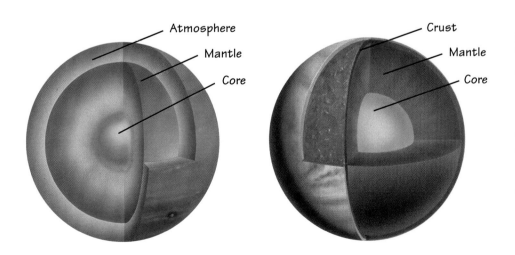

Atmosphere
Mantle
Core

Crust
Mantle
Core

The cores of a gas giant planet and a terrestrial planet *differ in relative size. Neptune (far left) has a much smaller core compared to its total size and a much larger mantle and a deeper atmosphere than Venus (near left) has. The two planets are not shown to scale here.*

Huge gas clouds, like the one shown here, may be the birthplace not only of stars but also of planetary systems, which form from the dust surrounding new stars.

Planetary Systems

A planetary system is a group of planets orbiting around a star or stars. Our solar system is a planetary system made up of one star, nine planets, asteroids, comets, and dust.

Are there other planetary systems in the universe? Some scientists claim that one star out of every ten may have planets. But the feeble glow of their reflected light is impossible to see from Earth.

To find these worlds, scientists look for other telltale signs. One is the way light shines from a star. If a star sometimes grows dimmer, this may be due to a planet passing between that star and Earth.

A planet can also make a star wobble a bit as its gravity tugs on the star. Scientists who chart a star's motion can detect tiny wobbles. They can also find a wobble by studying a star's light. Its light will look redder when the star is moving away from Earth and bluer when the star is moving toward Earth—a variation called the Doppler shift. The Doppler shift also helps scientists figure out what a planet is like. A big planet, or a planet that is close to a star, will cause a bigger Doppler shift.

In 1995, scientists used the Doppler shift to find the first large planet outside our solar system. Such a planet is called an extrasolar planet. The new planet orbits a star called 51 Pegasi in the constellation Pegasus.

Planet 51 Pegasi B seems to be a gas giant planet with half the mass of Jupiter. It is closer to its star than Mercury is to the Sun. At this distance, 51 Pegasi B takes only about four Earth days to orbit once.

In the years following the discovery of 51 Pegasi B, many more extrasolar planets were found. Three of them orbit one star. Astronomers expected these planets to be similar to the ones in our solar system: rocky planets close to a star, with gas giant planets farther out, all traveling in nearly circular orbits.

Instead, many of the new planets are as big as or bigger than Jupiter and orbit close to the stars. Others have long, elliptical orbits, making them swoop close to their stars, then swing far away. These discoveries are forcing astronomers to rethink how planetary systems form.

For example, scientists have long believed that gas giant planets could not form too close to a star. There would not be enough dust and gas near the center of a hot, new solar system to form a huge planet. Such planets could only form farther from the star, where there are larger amounts of material. But most of the extrasolar planets we have found are very big and very close to their stars.

One new theory to explain this is based on the idea of planet-eating stars. It states that stars may sometimes swallow small, new planets that are close to them. This happens when small planets travel too slowly to escape a star's gravity. The small planets may have slowed down because a big planet was tugging on them as it orbited farther out. In a way, the big planet shoved the little planets into the star.

The big planet, however, was also slowed down—not by another planet, but by a dust and gas cloud lying beyond its orbit. As it slowed, it moved closer to its star, just like the small planets.

Another theory tries to explain the orbits of the new planets. It states that the new planets may have started out in nearly circular orbits like Earth's. But two or more planets may have come too close to each other. The tugging of their gravity may have caused one planet to be kicked out of its planetary system. The other planet's orbit might also have been squashed into a long ellipse. So far, only one extrasolar planet has a nearly circular orbit.

Astronomers have found a Jupiter-size planet orbiting a small star called Gliese 876. This star is a red dwarf star, much smaller than our Sun. The new planet is the first to be found orbiting a red dwarf. If there are planets orbiting other red dwarfs, then the galaxy may be full of planets—because red dwarf stars are the most common stars in the universe.

So far, scientists have only found planets that rival Jupiter in size, because Earth-size planets are harder to locate. They barely make their stars wobble. Such small Doppler shifts are difficult to detect but future space telescopes should spot them.

So far, we have not actually seen these new planets. In 1998, however, the Hubble Space Telescope photographed a space object called TMR-IC. It may be an extrasolar planet that was flung out of its planetary system into space. *SEE ALSO GAS GIANT PLANETS; SOLAR NEBULA; SOLAR SYSTEM; TERRESTRIAL PLANETS.*

THE EXPLOSIVE BIRTH OF A PLANETARY SYSTEM

Many astronomers believe that planetary systems begin when huge old stars (1) explode as supernovas (2). Heavy elements, such as carbon, lithium, and beryllium, fly out into interstellar space and mix with abundant hydrogen gas there. It was from such a supernova soup that the solar system may have formed almost 5 billion years ago. After expanding, the nebula (cloud) of gas began to cool, contract, and spin faster. Most of the matter settled into the center. As pressure increased there, an atomic reaction began, and the sun was born (3). Farther from the center, where temperatures were cooler, gases solidified into grains of matter. Bits and pieces collided, clumped together, and eventually formed the planets (4).

Planets of the Solar System

Long before the telescope was invented, humans studied the night sky. They noticed that the stars rose and set, just as the Sun did. They also noticed that most stars did not move in relation to each other. A few points of light, however, traveled across the sky, moving from one group of stars to another and sometimes even backtracking.

These strange stars became known as wanderers, or planets. The word *planet* comes from a Greek word meaning "wanderer." Later, humans discovered that the planets do not wander aimlessly in space but follow fixed orbits around the Sun.

Earth is one of nine planets in our solar system. From the Sun outward, these planets are Mercury, Venus, Earth, Mars, Jupiter, Saturn, Uranus, Neptune, and Pluto. Pluto's orbit sometimes brings it closer to the Sun than Neptune, however.

It takes the Sun's light about eight minutes to reach Earth as it travels a distance of about 150 million kilometers (93 million miles). If you could fly to the Sun on a jet moving at the speed of sound, it would take you about 14 years. If you headed in the opposite direction and flew that jet to Pluto, the farthest planet, your trip would last about 550 years.

The four gas giant planets (Jupiter, Saturn, Uranus, and Neptune) dwarf Pluto and the inner planets (Mercury, Venus, Earth, and Mars), but are insignificant next to the Sun (partly visible, top).

Huge distances separate the planets, but they also share many features. For example, all the planets travel around the Sun in a counterclockwise direction. They orbit in paths called ellipses. These ellipses are nearly, but not quite, circular.

All the planets also spin, or rotate, as they orbit. This rotating is what makes the Sun seem to rise in the east in our sky and set in the west. All the planets rotate counterclockwise except for Venus, which revolves clockwise, and Uranus and Pluto, which spin on their sides like wheels. Venus also lacks moons, as does Mercury. But all the rest of the planets have one or more moons.

Like stars, planets shine in the night sky. But unlike stars, they do not give off their own light. Planets reflect the Sun's light. Planets do not burn and glow because they do not have nuclear fusion reactions taking place inside them as stars do.

Planets are also much smaller than stars. Even Jupiter, which could hold over 1,000 Earths, is tiny compared to a star. Over 99 percent of the material in our solar system is contained by the Sun.

Our solar system's planets are divided into two groups and one lone planet: terrestrial planets, gas giant planets, and Pluto. The terrestrial planets are closest to the Sun. They are Mercury, Venus, Earth, and Mars. The terrestrial planets are also known as "rocky" planets. They are all small planets made of rock, with thin atmospheres (except for Mercury, which has no atmosphere at all).

Between Mars and Jupiter lies the asteroid belt. It marks the border between the terrestrial planets and the gas giant planets. This belt is like a junk-yard filled with chunks of rock and ice. Although some asteroids are so big they are known as "minor planets," they are pebbles compared to Jupiter.

Jupiter, the largest planet, is one of four gas giant planets. Saturn, Uranus, and Neptune are the others. All four are huge planets with very deep atmospheres and relatively small cores of rock. Their atmospheres hold much hydrogen and helium. These gases also exist in liquid form on the gas giant planets. The gas planets are much colder than the terrestrial ones. Each gas giant planet has rings of rock and ice orbiting it as well as many moons. Saturn's rings are the most spectacular.

The Pluto-Kuiper Express spacecraft *will reach Pluto and its moon, Charon, in 2012 after a nine-year journey. It will map the surfaces of the pair and analyze their atmospheres.*

The oddball planet in our solar system is Pluto. Pluto is the smallest planet. Icy and rocky, it rotates slowly like a terrestrial planet but lies in the region of the gas giant planets. Its orbit is strange, too. All the other planets orbit the Sun in the same plane. You can imagine them as sitting on a giant compact disc that spins around the Sun. Pluto, however, rises above the disk, then sinks below it as it travels around the Sun, and its orbit is not as circular as the orbits of the other planets.

Many scientists think Pluto may be an object that escaped being caught by Neptune's gravity and becoming one of its moons. Other scientists do not consider Pluto to be a planet. They say that Pluto is more like an asteroid or a burned-out comet.

Some scientists believe that there is yet another planet beyond Pluto—a tenth planet in our solar system, which scientists call Planet X.

Planet X has a long history. Astronomers began looking for a Planet X in the 1800s when they noticed that Uranus did not follow its orbit exactly as it should. It seemed that something was pulling Uranus off its path a bit. The only thing that could be causing this odd behavior was another planet.

The first Planet X to be discovered was Neptune in 1841. But Neptune turned out not to be the cause of Uranus's wobble. In fact, Neptune had its own wobble. Pluto, the next Planet X, was discovered in 1930. But it was too small to cause the wobbling.

At this time, Uranus and Neptune no longer seem to wobble. But some scientists say things might have been different 200 years ago. According to this theory, there is a Planet X that takes 1,000 years to orbit the Sun. It travels at a very steep angle in a very long, elliptical orbit. When Planet X is close, it disturbs some planets' orbits. When it is far away, it does not. Other scientists state that perhaps big objects in the Kuiper Belt (an area stretching from Neptune to beyond Pluto) may sometimes cause planets to wobble. Still others say the idea of Planet X is nonsense and that the wobbles were just mathematical errors.

Space probes may someday solve this mystery. So far, probes have visited all the planets except Pluto. Lonely Pluto, however, may finally receive a visitor from Earth in 2012 when the *Pluto-Kuiper Express* is scheduled to arrive. After surveying Pluto and its moon, Charon, the spacecraft will head out into the Kuiper Belt to study chunks of ice and rock.

SEE ALSO GAS GIANT PLANETS; SOLAR SYSTEM; TERRESTRIAL PLANETS.

Pluto

In Roman mythology, Pluto is the god of the under-world—the world of the dead. In astronomy, Pluto is the ninth planet—a cold chunk of rock and ice orbiting 5.91 billion kilometers (3.67 billion miles) from the Sun at the solar system's outer edge.

Nobody knew of Pluto's existence until February 18, 1930. On that day, an astronomer named Clyde Tombaugh noticed it in a pair of photographs taken with the same telescope on two different nights. All the points of light in each photo shone in the same places except for one tiny spot that had moved across the sky. That spot was Pluto.

The smallest planet in our solar system, Pluto is only two-thirds the size of our Moon. Pluto's moon, in turn, is half Pluto's size. Discovered in

Charon looms over Pluto *in this painting of our most distant planet and its moon. From Pluto the Sun appears as a very bright star.*

1978, it was named Charon after the ferryman in Greek mythology who brings the dead to Pluto's underworld. It takes 6.4 days for Charon to complete its orbit around Pluto—the time it takes Pluto to spin once on its axis. As a result, Charon is always on the same side of Pluto and always presents the same face to Pluto. Similarly, our Moon always presents the same face to us (we never see its far side). If you lived on the far side of Pluto, the side that faces away from Charon, you would never see the moon.

Some scientists don't consider Pluto to be a planet at all. They think it may be an object from the

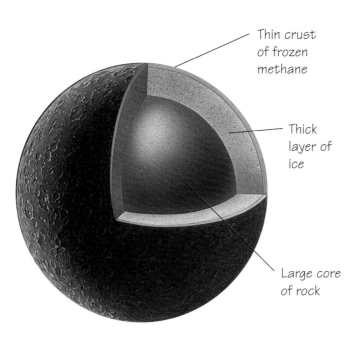

Thin crust of frozen methane

Thick layer of ice

Large core of rock

Scientists think Pluto's inner structure may consist of three layers: a thin crust of frozen methane covering a thick layer of ice wrapped around a large central core of rock.

PLUTO Fast Facts

Mass: 0.002 x Earth
Volume: 0.006 x Earth
Diameter at equator: 2,300 kilometers (1,430 miles). Smallest planet
Distance from Sun: 5,915 billion kilometers (3,676.2 billion miles). Farthest planet from Sun
Moons: 1
Average temperature: -233°C (-419°F)
Time to rotate on axis: 6.4 days
Time to orbit Sun: 248 years
Rings: No
Atmosphere: Nitrogen, methane

Did You Know? Most of the time, Pluto is the farthest planet from the Sun, but sometimes it is the second farthest planet—when its orbit crosses inside Neptune's orbit.

Kuiper Belt, a zone stretching from Neptune to beyond Pluto that holds chunks of planetary material, ice, and comets leftover from the formation of the solar system. Pluto is very similar to Neptune's largest moon, Triton. It may be that long ago both Pluto and Triton orbited the Sun independently. Triton may have been caught in Neptune's gravity, but Pluto may never have been close enough to Neptune to be trapped.

Pluto and Neptune, the two outermost planets, do sometimes cross paths, but they never come close to colliding. Pluto's orbit is tilted and also much more elliptical than the orbits of the other eight planets. This causes Pluto to travel inside of Neptune's orbital path, temporarily making Neptune the farthest planet from the Sun. Neptune held this position for 20 years—from February 7, 1979 to February 11, 1999, when Pluto crossed beyond Neptune's orbit once again. Pluto will remain the farthest planet until the year 2227.

Because Pluto's orbit is extremely elliptical, the planet is nearly twice as far from the Sun at its far-thest point than it is at its closest point. During half of its 248-year orbit Pluto is so cold that the nitrogen and methane in its thin atmosphere freezes and forms frost on the planet's surface. When Pluto moves closer to the Sun for the other 124 years, the Sun's heat makes the frost evaporate into the atmosphere again.

Like Uranus, Pluto is a planet tipped on its side. Scientists speculate that Pluto could have crashed into an object big enough to push it over and to knock material out of Pluto to form Charon.

The Hubble Space Telescope's images of Pluto have brought us much new information, but the planet is still a mystery. That will change if the *Pluto-Kuiper Express* takes off as planned in 2003 or 2004. Its first mission will be to explore the surfaces of Pluto and Charon. Then it will fly on to a newly discovered area called the Edgeworth-Kuiper Disk to study "ice dwarfs," chunks of material that may hold clues about how Earth's atmosphere and life formed. The *Pluto-Kuiper Express* is expected to reach Pluto in 2012 or later—less than 100 years after the discovery of this lonely planet. *SEE ALSO CHARON; COMETS; PLANETS OF THE SOLAR SYSTEM.*

Ptolemy

Ptolemy (100?–170?) was a Greek astronomer and mathematician who created an early model of how the solar system worked. People accepted this model for more than 1,000 years, but it was not correct.

Ptolemy's 13 volumes on astronomy were used as textbooks for 1,400 years.

Ptolemy believed the Earth stood still at the center of the universe. Many people thought this was true at the time and also thought that stars and planets traveled in perfect circles around Earth. But there was a problem with these ideas. Planets sometimes seemed to move backward. Also, the Moon and planets seemed to change in brightness and size.

Ptolemy developed a theory to explain such odd events. He said that the Sun, Moon, and planets traveled in little circles as they went around in big circles. In a way, they "looped the loop" as they orbited Earth.

This model of the solar system is called the Ptolemaic System. It ruled astronomy until 1543, when a book by astronomer Nicolaus Copernicus was published. Copernicus believed what we now know to be true: that the planets revolve around the Sun, not Earth. SEE ALSO COPERNICUS, NICOLAUS; GALILEO; KEPLER, JOHANNES.

Ride, Sally

Sally Ride (1951–), an astronaut and physicist, was the first American woman in space. She made her historic flight aboard the space shuttle *Challenger*, which blasted off from the Kennedy Space Center on June 18, 1983. Ride's job title was Mission Specialist. She worked with other crew members to put two satellites in orbit during a week-long mission.

Ride was only 12 years old when the first woman went into space. That woman was Valentina Tereshkova, a Soviet cosmonaut. She rocketed into space in a capsule called *Vostok 6* in June 1963. Tereshkova orbited Earth for three days. SEE ALSO ASTRONAUTS AND COSMONAUTS; SPACE SHUTTLE.

Rotation

Rotation is the spinning of a planet, stars, moon, or other space object around an axis. Galaxies rotate, too. The Sun rotates in a counterclockwise direction, taking 25 days at its equator to spin around once. The planets follow the Sun's lead and orbit it in a counterclockwise direction. As they orbit, they spin.

Most of the planets spin in a counterclockwise direction; Venus, Uranus, and Pluto do not. Venus

Sally Ride got her job as an astronaut after reading an ad in the newspaper. She was one of 35 women selected from among the 1,251 who applied.

spins clockwise. On Venus, the Sun would rise in the west and set in the east. Uranus and Pluto spin on their sides like wheels instead of like tops. The Sun shines directly on their north or south poles.

Venus takes the longest to spin around once. It rotates once every 243 days—18 days longer than it takes to orbit the Sun! Jupiter, the biggest planet, spins the fastest. It takes only 9 hours and 54 minutes to rotate once. It spins so quickly that its middle bulges and its clouds stretch out in wide, colorful stripes.

Moons rotate as they orbit their planets, too. Most of them keep the same sides facing their planets. The planets' gravity pulls strongly on their moons, forcing them to slow their spin until they are rotating once in the same amount of time it takes them to orbit their planet once.

Saturn's little moon Hyperion is one moon that does not follow this rule, however. It does not always show the same side to Saturn. Its rotation rate changes as time goes by, and it seems to be tumbling as it travels. Scientists think the big Saturn moon Titan tugs on Hyperion and helps cause its weird motion. Hyperion may also have been hit by a large space object in the past.

The planets' motions are due to the formation of the solar system. The solar system is believed to have formed from a huge, spinning cloud of gas and dust. As the gas and dust clumped toward the center of this cloud, it spun faster—just as a skater spins faster if he twirls with his arms tucked in at his sides instead of stretched out. When the planets formed, they all spun like tops in the same counterclockwise direction as the gas-dust cloud.

But the young planets often collided with large chunks of rock as they formed. Some planets, such as Earth, were knocked into a tilt by these crashes. Uranus was completely bowled over onto its side. A crash may explain Venus's odd rotation, too. SEE ALSO PLANETARY SYSTEMS.

Sagan, Carl

Carl Sagan (1934–1997) was an American astronomer who studied the possibility of life on other planets. His work made other scientists take the search for life in outer space seriously. This branch of the life sciences is now called exobiology.

Sagan helped plan the journeys of the *Mariner*, *Viking*, *Voyager*, and *Galileo* spacecraft. He also helped create the messages that rode into space with the space probes *Pioneer 10* and *Pioneer 11*. These messages include diagrams of Earth's location in space, an atom of hydrogen, and what human beings look like.

Sagan popularized the theory of nuclear winter. This theory states that a nuclear war could fill Earth's atmosphere with dust, blocking the Sun's light and causing worldwide freezing. Sagan studied Venus and suggested that this hot planet suffered from global warming caused by the greenhouse effect. Scientists today are studying the greenhouse effect and possible global warming here on Earth.

Sagan became world-famous when he produced and starred in a popular series on television in 1980 called *Cosmos*. This series told the story of astronomy and took viewers on a voyage through time and space. Sagan wrote many books. One was a novel entitled *Contact*, which was made into a movie. SEE ALSO GREENHOUSE EFFECT; PIONEER PROGRAM.

Carl Sagan said the idea that only our planet supports life is as wrong as early beliefs that Earth was the center of the universe.

solar system, has a spectacular ring system around it. The black spot below the rings is the shadow of Tethys, Saturn's closest moon. Two other moons, Dione and Rhea, are visible as tiny white spots in the lower right of this true-color photo taken by Voyager 2 in 1981 from a distance of 21 million kilometers (13 million miles).

Saturn

Thousands of rings encircle Saturn, the sixth planet from the Sun. You can observe this ring system, which is 400,000 kilometers (250,000 miles) wide, through an ordinary store-bought telescope. Though the rings are wide, they are surprisingly thin. In some areas, the ring system is just 10 meters (33 feet) thick—about the length of a school bus. In the thickest areas, it is only 1.5 kilometers (.93 miles) thick.

For centuries, people believed that Saturn was the only planet with rings. Now we know that Jupiter, Uranus, and Neptune—the other planets made mostly of gases—are also ringed. It was also believed that only three rings circled Saturn. In 1980 the *Voyager 1* spacecraft flew past Saturn followed in 1981 by *Voyager 2*, and they astonished everyone with their discoveries. The spacecrafts sent back photographs showing that each ring held hundreds of ringlets. Each ringlet is made up of ice-coated rocks ranging in size from a pebble to a house. Some chunks may even be up to 1 kilometer (one-half mile) wide. Scientists group these ringlets into seven main rings.

It is not known where the rocks in the ringlets came from. They may be particles of moons that crashed into each other, or they may be the remains of moons or comets that came too close to Saturn and were trapped and ripped apart by its gravity.

As of 1999, scientists counted 18 moons orbiting Saturn, and they think more will be discovered. Some moons prevent material from escaping the rings. They are called "shepherd satellites" because they "herd" the particles into rings.

Like Jupiter, Saturn is a gas giant planet. It is made mostly of hydrogen. Layers of clouds float in an atmosphere that is mostly hydrogen gas. Below the atmosphere is a layer of liquid hydrogen, which surrounds a layer of metallic, liquid hydrogen and helium. Buried deep inside is Saturn's red-hot, semi-solid core.

Saturn is nearly as big as Jupiter, but it is much less dense. This means a box filled with the matter that makes up Saturn would hold less material than a same-size box of Jupiter's matter. Saturn is the only planet less dense than water. If you could build a pool big enough to contain Saturn, it would float on the water's surface. Jupiter and the other planets would sink.

Saturn is not as stormy as Jupiter, although red and blue storm spots swirl in its clouds. Its winds, however, race much faster. Some winds on Saturn

SATURN Fast Facts

Mass: 95 × Earth
Volume: 764 × Earth
Diameter at equator: 120,536 kilometers (74,853 miles). Second largest planet
Distance from Sun: 1,427 million kilometers (886 million miles)
Moons: 18 known
Average temperature: -139°C (-218°F)
Time to rotate on axis at equator: 10 hours, 30 minutes
Time to orbit Sun: 29.5 years
Rings: Yes
Atmosphere: Hydrogen, helium

DID YOU KNOW?
Saturn's north and south poles glow with ultraviolet displays, called auroras, when the solar wind whips past the planet. They are similar to Earth's auroras.

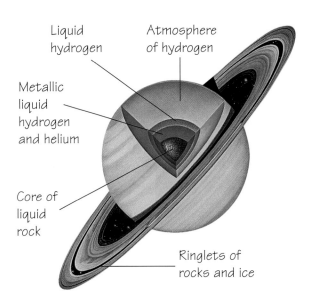

Liquid hydrogen
Atmosphere of hydrogen
Metallic liquid hydrogen and helium
Core of liquid rock
Ringlets of rocks and ice

A giant globe made mostly of gases, Saturn is ringed by trillions of ice and rock particles. Electrical currents in a layer of metallic hydrogen and helium create a magnetic field. The liquid-rock core weighs as much as a dozen Earths.

have been clocked at 1,800 kilometers (1,100 miles) per hour—ten times as fast as a hurricane on Earth. In 1990, the Hubble Space Telescope took a photo of Saturn showing that a giant white spot had appeared near the equator. The spot was a massive storm filled with clouds of ammonia—the same substance we use in floor cleaners.

One day on Saturn lasts 10 hours and 30 minutes—about 36 minutes longer than a day on Jupiter. But Saturn is twice as far from the Sun as Jupiter, and it takes the ringed planet nearly 30 years to orbit the Sun—more than twice as long as it takes Jupiter to complete its trip around the Sun.

On October 15, 1997, the spacecraft *Cassini* blasted off from Cape Canaveral, Florida, to start its long voyage to Saturn—a trip that will take nearly seven years. When *Cassini* arrives at the ringed planet in 2004, it will start a four-year mission of scientific exploration. SEE ALSO GAS GIANT PLANETS; MIMAS; MOONS OF THE PLANETS; TITAN; VOYAGER MISSION.

Seasons

Seasons are weather changes that happen as planets move in their orbits around the Sun.

There are four seasons in most parts of the northern hemisphere, or half, of Earth. They are spring, summer, autumn, and winter. Many places in the southern hemisphere have these four seasons, too, but their seasons are the opposite: when it is winter in North America, for example, it is summer in South America. Many areas along the equator have just two seasons—a wet season and a dry one.

To understand how Earth's seasons happen, first imagine Earth as a ball with a stick through its middle running from the north pole to the south pole. This stick is Earth's axis. Earth spins around its axis. But its axis does not stand up straight like a flagpole. Instead, it is tilted. If you look at a globe, you will see that it spins at a tilt, too. It is this tilt that causes seasons.

Now imagine this tilted Earth orbiting the Sun. For part of this orbit, the northern hemisphere is tipped toward the Sun. It gets more light and heat from the Sun this way. This is partly because the Sun's rays hit it directly. Also, the northern hemisphere spends more time in sunlight. So the days are longer than the nights. At the north pole, the Sun never really sets. It is summer in the north.

All the planets tilt on their axes *except Mercury, so most planets experience seasons of some kind. Uranus and Pluto rotate practically on their sides. Venus and Jupiter have slight tilts. The remaining planets have tilts similar to Earth's.*

Meanwhile, the southern hemisphere is tipped away from the Sun. Days are shorter there. The Sun's light hits the south at an angle instead of straight on. So this half of Earth gets less light and heat. It is winter in the south.

A half-year later, this scene is reversed. Now the southern hemisphere is tipped toward the Sun, and the northern hemisphere is tipped away. The south enjoys summer while the north experiences winter. At the north pole, the Sun doesn't even rise.

Spring and autumn are in-between seasons. On March 21 and on September 21 (the vernal and autumnal equinox), day and night are the same length. *Equinox* means "equal night."

The longest day of the year in the northern hemisphere usually falls on June 21. It is called the summer solstice. The shortest day falls on or around December 21. This is the winter solstice.

Equinoxes and solstices mark the first official days of the seasons. SEE ALSO ORBIT; ROTATION.

Solar Eclipse

When the Moon passes in front of the Sun and blocks its light from Earth, we see a solar eclipse. *Solar* means "of the sun." *To eclipse* means "to darken."

How can the Moon block the Sun? The Moon is quite small; the Sun is gigantic. The Moon can block the Sun's light because it is so much closer to Earth than the Sun, and so it appears to be nearly the same size. You can see how this works by extending your arm in front of you and holding up your thumb to block an object from your view. You

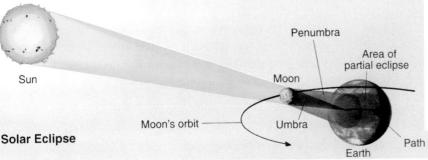

Solar Eclipse

Sun

Penumbra

Moon

Moon's orbit

Umbra

Area of partial eclipse

Earth

Path of totality

*A **solar eclipse** occurs when the Moon passes between Earth and the Sun, blocking the Sun's light from Earth and casting a shadow (umbra) on Earth. Solar eclipses reveal solar flares (below, left) and striking effects such as the diamond ring (below, right).*

can probably cover a building or a tall tree in the distance with your thumb in this way. Yet your thumb is nowhere near as large as the object it is blocking!

A total solar eclipse occurs when the Moon, the Sun, and Earth are lined up in a row, with the Moon between the Sun and Earth. The Moon must also be at the closest point to Earth in its orbit. When this happens, the Moon moves in front of the Sun. It blocks its light completely. All that shines around the Moon is the dim light of the Sun's corona (the top layer of the Sun's atmosphere). The sky grows dark. Planets and stars appear. Birds fall silent as the Moon's shadow crosses Earth.

The path of this shadow is narrow so each solar eclipse is seen in only a small part of the world. People living at the edges of the path see a partial solar eclipse. A partial solar eclipse occurs when the Earth, Moon, and Sun are not in an exact line. An annular eclipse occurs when the Moon isn't at its closest point to Earth but the two are lined up with the Sun. Then the Sun's disk is visible as a ring around the Moon.

You must never look directly at the Sun during a solar eclipse. Even when it is behind the Moon, the Sun sends out radiation that is strong enough to cause blindness. It is much safer to look at photographs to see the special effects of a solar eclipse.

One special effect is called Baily's beads. This is a winking row of bright lights made when the Sun shines through mountains along the edge of the Moon. Another is the diamond ring. This is a burst of light on a thin glowing ring that appears around the Moon, just before and after it blocks out the Sun. SEE ALSO LUNAR ECLIPSE; MOON; SUN.

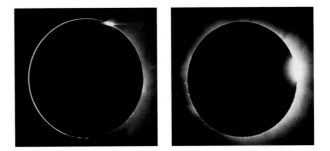

Solar Nebula

The solar nebula was the huge cloud of dust and gas that became our solar system 4.6 billion years ago.

Scientists think that the cloud began to fall in on itself as its particles attracted each other with their gravity. A nearby exploding star may have given this collapse an extra push. As the cloud collapsed, it began to spin faster and faster—just as ice skaters spin faster when they twirl with their arms spread out and then tuck them in.

Gravity made the particles crash into each other, and sometimes they stuck together. Over time, they formed bigger and bigger chunks of rock. Gases were attracted to these chunks, too.

The early Sun sat at the center of the spinning, flattened cloud. It was a protostar, a ball of gases and some metals. As it grew larger and pressure built up inside, its core became hot enough to squeeze hydrogen atoms together to make helium in a reaction called nuclear fusion. The protostar was now a burning star, shining on objects called protoplanets—the objects that would one day be planets. SEE ALSO PLANETARY SYSTEMS; STAR; SUN; UNIVERSE.

Solar System

A solar system is made up of a star and the space objects that orbit it. These objects may include planets, asteroids, meteoroids, and comets.

The center of our solar system is the Sun. The Sun is an ordinary star but special for us because it is our star. Its energy fuels most life on Earth. In the galaxy, however, it is just one of many "yellow" stars.

Orbiting the Sun are nine planets. They are Mercury, Venus, Earth, Mars, Jupiter, Saturn, Uranus, Neptune, and Pluto. Mercury is closest to the Sun. Pluto is usually the farthest away. Its odd orbit makes it move closer to the Sun than Neptune every 228 years. All of the planets orbit the Sun in a counterclockwise direction.

Also in orbit around the Sun are chunks of rock called asteroids. Most of them lie in a zone between Mars and Jupiter. Meteoroids are small fragments from asteroids and comets that orbit in many places. Chunks of ice and rock called comets orbit the Sun, too. Some comets come from the Kuiper Belt, which lies just beyond Neptune. Many of them come from a zone beyond Pluto called the Oort Cloud.

The Oort Cloud is part of our solar system. It surrounds the solar system like a giant ball and reaches one-sixteenth of the way toward Proxima Centauri, the nearest star to the Sun. The Voyager space probes, which crossed Pluto's orbit in 1990, will not reach the outer edge of the Oort Cloud for almost 10,000 years.

How did the solar system form? It is believed that about 4.6 billion years ago, a huge cloud of gas and dust began to form clumps in its center and spin. An exploding star nearby may have caused the cloud to collapse and spin in this way. As the central clump grew, it attracted more material and grew even bigger. The bigger it got, the hotter it became. The pressure inside it rose, too. It became a protostar—a kind of space egg waiting to hatch into a full-blown star.

Finally, the protostar grew so big that a nuclear reaction began. Hydrogen atoms began squashing together to make helium. This reaction gave off energy in the form of heat and light. The protostar was now a burning star.

Meanwhile, some of the dust and gas whirling around the protostar was clumping together, too. These clumps became plantesimals—planets-in-the-making. The ones nearest the hot protostar contained much rocky material. The ones farther away had less rocky material but more gas and ice. The plantesimals grew into planets over a span of 100 million years.

Earth and the other planets began forming about 4.6 billion years ago. Our solar system will most likely survive for another 5 billion years. Then the Sun will begin to burn out, and the solar system as we know it will come to an end.

Are there other solar systems? The Milky Way galaxy alone contains 100 billion stars or more. We have recently discovered that other planets do orbit

Our solar system consists of the Sun, the nine planets and their moons, asteroids, comets, and meteoroids, plus gases, dust, and other material left over from the time the solar system formed.

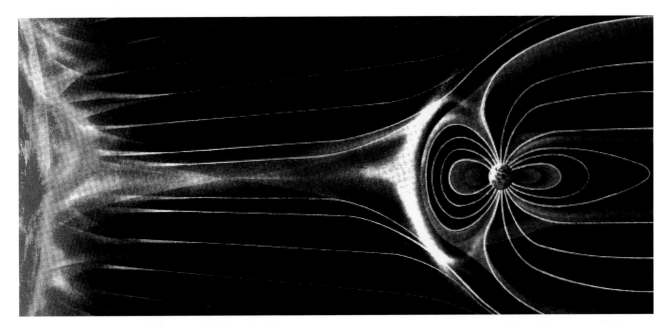

stars. The first was discovered in 1995. In 1999 scientists discovered three big planets orbiting a single star, proof that other solar systems exist. To date, though, we can detect only planets that are at least as big as Jupiter. Jupiter is the largest planet in our solar system. Someday we will surely be able to find smaller planets.

In the meantime, scientists are studying other galaxies and clouds of dust called nebulae. Here they hope to find clues to the past to help us learn more about our solar system's beginnings. *SEE ALSO GAS GIANT PLANETS; PLANETARY SYSTEMS; PLANETS OF THE SOLAR SYSTEM; TERRESTRIAL PLANETS.*

Solar Wind

The solar wind is a stream of particles that flows from the Sun. These particles carry a strong electrical charge. They are called ions. The solar wind also carries a magnetic field.

The solar wind escapes from the Sun through areas called coronal holes where the Sun's magnetic field is relatively weak. These are places where the Sun's magnetic field loops high above the Sun's atmosphere.

It takes about five days for the solar wind to reach Earth. By the time the wind sweeps past our planet, it is traveling at 700 kilometers (435 miles)

A continuous stream of atomic particles, called the solar wind, flows into space from the Sun's surface. Most of these particles are pushed away from Earth by our planet's magnetic field. Some particles, however, reach the upper atmosphere and cause radio interference and brilliant light displays known as the aurora borealis (northern lights) and aurora australis (southern lights).

per second. This hot, fast blast from the Sun would eventually wipe out life on Earth if it hit the planet. But Earth is protected by its magnetosphere. The magnetosphere is like a magnetic bubble around Earth. It forces the solar wind to sweep around Earth and over its north and south poles.

Sometimes we can see the solar wind reacting with Earth's magnetic field. This reaction causes colorful, glowing lights, called auroras, to flicker in the sky above the north and south poles. You are also witnessing the solar wind at work when you see a comet. It is the solar wind that blows the comet's dust and gas into the shape of a tail.

The solar wind doesn't stop at Pluto. It flows far out into space. There it meets the interstellar wind. This wind stops the solar wind at a place called the heliopause. Scientists think the heliopause lies in an area 120 times the distance between the Sun and Earth. *SEE ALSO AURORA; MAGNETIC FIELDS; SOLAR SYSTEM; SUN; VAN ALLEN BELTS.*

Belching fire and smoke, the U.S. space shuttle Discovery lifts off from Cape Canaveral on January 16, 1995. The orbiter is attached to a silo-sized liquid fuel tank and two solid rocket boosters.

Eileen Collins was the first woman to pilot a space shuttle (February 1995) and the first woman to command a space shuttle mission (July 1999).

Space Shuttle

The space shuttle can be launched and used for space travel many times. After taking off like a rocket, it orbits Earth like a satellite, then reenters the atmosphere and soars to a landing on a runway like a glider. While in space, the shuttle crew launches new satellites or fixes ones already in orbit. They can even bring ailing satellites back to Earth in the orbiter's huge cargo bay. Shuttles also carry scientific experiments into space.

A space shuttle is made up of an orbiter, an external fuel tank, and a pair of solid rocket boosters. The orbiter is 37 meters (122 feet) and looks like a jet. It's attached to the external fuel tank, a giant orange silo 46 meters (154 feet) long. On either side of the tank stand the solid rocket boosters.

At launch time, fuel from the external tank gushes into the orbiter's three main engines and ignites. The solid fuel in the boosters ignites, too. Then the shuttle rockets upward on a pillar of flame.

About two minutes after lift-off, the boosters drop off, their fuel spent. Parachutes slow their fall into the ocean, where ships retrieve them to be used again. Nearly seven minutes later, the external tank falls away and burns up as it plunges through the atmosphere.

The orbiter circles Earth 16 times a day at 25,000 kilometers (17,500 miles) per hour, crossing North America in just 10 minutes. As the orbiter reenters Earth's atmosphere, its surface heats up to about 1,400°C (2,500°F). Over 20,000 heat tiles shield the orbiter from this red-hot welcome home. Finally, it lands on a runway 5 kilometers (3 miles) long.

The first shuttle, *Columbia*, lifted off on April 12, 1981. It is still in use today, along with three others—*Discovery*, *Atlantis*, and *Endeavour*. On January 28, 1986, a fifth shuttle (named *Challenger*) exploded shortly after lift-off. This terrible accident stopped the shuttle program for over two years while experts worked to redesign the shuttle's rocket boosters and make them safer. SEE ALSO ASTRONAUTS AND COSMONAUTS; EXPLORATION OF THE SOLAR SYSTEM; RIDE, SALLY; SPACE STATION.

Space Station

A space station is a workplace in space that orbits Earth as a satellite. Here, astronauts and cosmonauts live and work for months at a time. Supply ships visit and dock at the space station to deliver new equipment and swap crew members.

The first space station, *Salyut 1*, was launched on April 19, 1971, by the USSR. Over the next 11 years, six more Salyut stations were sent up.

Skylab, the first U.S. space station, began orbiting Earth on May 14, 1973. Almost 300 experiments were conducted on *Skylab*. Scientists learned much about the Earth, the Sun, and how weightlessness affects the human body. Then the station was abandoned. It fell out of orbit and crashed to Earth, scattering pieces in western Australia and the Indian Ocean.

The first section of the Russian space station *Mir* was launched on February 20, 1986. More sections were added later. In 1996, U.S. astronaut Dr. Shannon W. Lucid spent 188 days and 5 hours on *Mir*, setting a U.S. record for time spent in space.

Beginning in 1998, sections of the International Space Station began to be launched into space. The United States, Russia, Brazil, Canada, Japan, and eleven European nations worked together to build it. This giant station is as large as two football fields. Six people can live on board for up to a year. SEE ALSO ASTRONAUTS AND COSMONAUTS; NASA; ORBIT; SPACE SHUTTLE.

A cosmonaut repairs the outside of Mir, the Russian space station launched in 1986. U.S. space shuttles docked with Mir in 1995, and astronauts joined the cosmonauts aboard.

Spectrum

The spectrum is the range of electromagnetic radiation produced by the objects in the universe. A rainbow is a display of the visible spectrum—the wavelengths of light that appear as colors to our eyes. Longer wavelengths include radio waves, microwaves, and infrared (heat) waves. Shorter wavelengths include ultraviolet radiation, gamma rays, and X rays. Astronomers study radiation to find out about planets, stars, black holes, and distant galaxies. SEE ALSO ATMOSPHERE; BLACK HOLE; NEWTON, SIR ISAAC; TELESCOPES; X RAYS.

Sputnik Series

On October 4, 1957, *Sputnik 1*, a radio satellite, became the first object successfully put into orbit. Launched from the USSR, it sent back information about the atmosphere and space. More important, it launched the space race—a competition that lasted 20 years between the United States and the USSR to outdo each other in space exploration. Ten Sputnik satellites in all were launched. *Sputnik 2* is famous for carrying the dog Laika, the first living creature, into orbit. SEE ALSO APOLLO PROGRAM; EXPLORATION OF THE SOLAR SYSTEM.

Stars vary enormously in size. Red supergiants are the largest stars. Neutron stars are the smallest. Our Sun is an average-size star—much larger than a white dwarf but much smaller than a red giant or a supergiant.

Supergiant

Red giant

Neutron star

Sun

White dwarfs

Star

A star is a huge spinning ball of burning gas—mostly hydrogen and helium gases and small amounts of other substances. Gravity holds the ball together. Pressure at the center is very great. Hydrogen atoms are squeezed together so tightly that they become very hot—at least 10,000,000°C (18,000,000°F)—and join to form helium in what is called a nuclear fusion reaction. Energy produced by this reaction travels slowly to the star's surface and is given off as heat and light.

A clear night sky glitters with thousands of stars, but these are just a handful of the more than 100 billion stars making up our galaxy.

Some young stars are many times bigger than our Sun. They are blue giants—very hot, bright stars with surface temperatures of around 25,000°C (45,000°F). When a blue giant runs out of hydrogen, it may puff up to 100 times its original size, then shrink to a tiny white dwarf star—a dim star not much bigger than Earth. Some bigger stars, however, blow up to form supergiant stars. A supergiant ends its life in a huge explosion called a supernova. A supernova can be so bright that it is visible from Earth in daylight.

A supernova's fireworks do not signal the end of the show. The material that flies out of the supernova and into space is just the outer layer of the dying star. It leaves a very dense, heavy core behind. This core can become a neutron star or a black hole. A neutron star is a small, heavy star that spins once per second or even faster. It can suck up material from nearby stars. A black hole is a very dense object with gravity so strong it can swallow light.

Most smaller stars die out more quietly. A star like the Sun may swell to be a red giant star and fling its outer layer into space, forming a cloud called a planetary nebula. All that remains behind is the core, a white dwarf. A white dwarf may be small—only about the size of the Earth—but so dense that just two teaspoons of it would weigh as much as an elephant. Eventually this star will fizzle out, becoming a black dwarf. SEE ALSO BLACK HOLE; CONSTELLATIONS; GALAXY; MILKY WAY GALAXY; SUN.

Sun

The Sun is a star like many others—a burning globe of mostly hydrogen and helium gases. Earth lies about 150 million kilometers (93 million miles) from the Sun. Sunlight takes about eight minutes to travel from the Sun to Earth.

Our Sun is a small star, but it is huge compared to the planets that orbit it. It is 1,390,000 kilometers (863,700 miles) wide. It would take 342 Earths strung together like a string of pearls to circle the Sun. The Sun could hold a million Earths inside it.

Like the planets, the Sun spins. But because it is made of gas, it does not spin evenly. The middle rotates in just 25 days; the north and south poles rotate once every 36 days.

Deep inside the Sun at its core, nuclear fusion takes place. Hydrogen atoms are squeezed together to make helium and energy. The temperature is believed to be about 15,000,000°C (27,000,000°F). It takes many thousands of years for this energy to flow to the Sun's surface.

The Sun's surface is about 5,500°C (10,000°F), much cooler than its core. Dark spots, called sunspots, make the surface look patchy. The Sun goes through 11-year sunspot cycles as the number and size of its spots grow and then drop again.

Above the surface is the Sun's atmosphere. The upper layer of the atmosphere is called the corona. It reaches out about 1.6 million kilometers (1 million miles) into space. It is much hotter than the Sun's surface—about 1,000,000°C (1,800,000°F).

The Sun's atmosphere is a stormy place. Strong magnetic fields move about on the Sun's surface. Giant loops of hot, electrically charged gas erupt. These loops are called prominences. Sharp spikes of gas called spicules also pierce the atmosphere. Sometimes, magnetic fields make areas of the Sun's atmosphere explode into space as bursts of energy called solar flares. They can interrupt radio commu-

SUN Fast Facts

Mass: 1.99 x 10³⁰ grams (333,000 x earth)
Volume: 1 million x Earth
Average surface temperature: 5,500°C (10,000°F)
Diameter at equator: 1,390,000 kilometers (863,700 miles)
Distance from Earth: 150 million kilometers (93 million miles)
Time to rotate on axis at equator: 25 days
Approximate age: 4.6 billion years

DID YOU KNOW?

Solar prominences are gigantic loops and tongues of glowing gas that can be as long as 600,000 kilometers (372,000 miles). Solar prominences may last for several months. At the end of their lives, solar prominences often shoot upwards and then fade out.

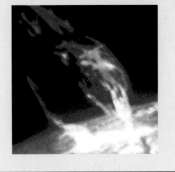

nication on Earth, confuse migrating birds, and even make electric garage doors fly open!

Scientists calculate that the Sun started shining about 4.6 billion years ago. It will burn for about another 5 billion years. Then it will start to die. First, it will swell and become a red giant. In the process, it will swallow up Mercury, Venus, and possibly Earth. Then its outer layers will drift into space while the core shrinks into a white dwarf.

The Sun is being closely studied by a space probe called SOHO, which stands for Solar and Heliospheric Observatory. Launched on December 2, 1995, SOHO is investigating the Sun inside and out. It is also finding out about the solar wind—a stream of electrically charged particles flowing from the Sun far out into space. With SOHO's help, scientists have discovered that tornadoes of hot, electrically charged gas about as wide as Earth whirl on the Sun's surface. It also found that the Sun suffers sunquakes. These quakes are caused by solar flares.

SEE ALSO SOLAR NEBULA; SOLAR WIND; STAR.

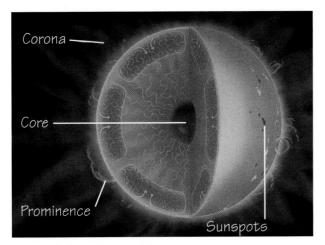

The Sun's light and heat come from its core, where hydrogen atoms are squeezed so tight that matter there is 14 times denser than lead.

Equipped with an AO system (AO stands for adaptive optics), the Shane Telescope (left) at the Lick Observatory in California produces pictures almost as sharp as those taken by the Hubble Space Telescope. An AO system uses computer-controlled, flexible mirrors and lasers to make up for the blurring effects of Earth's atmosphere. The two images at right show a star photographed with an AO system (a) and without it (b).

Telescopes

A telescope is an instrument that makes distant objects appear larger and closer. Optical telescopes use visible light, but some telescopes use other parts of the spectrum such as radio waves or X rays.

An optical telescope works by gathering light and focusing it. It has two main parts: an objective and an eyepiece. In reflecting telescopes the objective is a curved mirror; in refracting telescopes the objective is a curved piece of glass called a lens. The eyepiece is the part you look into. It holds one or more lenses and makes the image look bigger.

The first telescope was a spyglass made by a Dutch eyeglass maker named Hans Lippershey in 1608. Italian astronomer Galileo Galilei heard about it and built his own in 1609. He was the first person to use a telescope to study space.

Galileo's telescope was a refracting telescope. Like all refractors in his day and age, it made rainbow colors glow at the edges of the things he saw. Sir Isaac Newton built a reflecting telescope in 1668. It produced much sharper images.

A good backyard telescope will help you see the Moon's craters, Saturn's rings, and even other galaxies. A big telescope such as the Hale Telescope on Palomar Mountain in California can look much farther into space, making a dim star look one million times brighter to your eyes. The Hale's mirror is 5.1 meters (200 inches) wide. Even larger are the two Keck optical telescopes in Hawaii. Each telescope has a mirror 10 meters (394 inches) wide made up of 36 smaller mirrors. One of the world's largest telescopes is the Very Large Telescope (VLT) located in the Atacama desert of Chile. It consists of four telescopes, each one 8.2 meters (27 feet) wide, plus three smaller telescopes that can all work together.

Optical telescopes are usually built on mountaintops so that clouds, dust, and city lights don't interfere with their view. Telescopes are also launched into space. The Hubble Space Telescope orbits 596 kilometers (370 miles) above Earth.

Other kinds of telescopes help us see other kinds of radiation given off by space objects. Radio telescopes, for example, pick up radio waves. A famous radio telescope is the Very Large Array in New Mexico. It has 27 radio dishes. Each one is 25 meters (82 feet) wide. A computer coordinates the dishes so they work like one big telescope.

There are also space telescopes collecting ultraviolet light, gamma rays, X rays, and infrared rays. They could not do their job on Earth's surface because Earth's atmosphere blocks much of this radiation. Astronomers use these telescopes to learn more about black holes, galaxies, the Sun, and stars. SEE ALSO GALILEO; HUBBLE SPACE TELESCOPE.

Terrestrial Planets

A terrestrial planet is a planet made mostly of rock. The terrestrial planets are Mercury, Venus, Earth, and Mars. The word terrestrial means "like Earth." They are closer to the Sun than the four gas giant planets—Jupiter, Saturn, Uranus, and Neptune.

Venus and Mars have thin atmospheres, like Earth. Mercury does not have one at all. The gas giant planets have deep atmospheres. Earth's atmosphere is mainly nitrogen and oxygen. Venus and Mars have carbon dioxide atmospheres. The gas giant planets have hydrogen and helium atmospheres.

Terrestrial planets lost most of their hydrogen because their gravity is weaker than the gravity of the gas giant planets and could not hold on to the light hydrogen gas molecules as well. Terrestrial planets are also warmer than the gas giant planets. Heat makes gas molecules move faster and escape into space more easily. *SEE ALSO GAS GIANT PLANETS.*

Tides

A tide is the rise and fall of a body of water caused by the pull of a moon or a planet. On Earth, water is pulled by the Moon and Sun. At high tide, the ocean rises high on the beach. At low tide, the water drops back. In most places, there are two high tides and two low tides every day.

Tides occur because the Moon's and Sun's gravity tug on Earth and its water. The Moon is much smaller than the Sun, and its gravity is weaker. But it is the main cause of the tides because it is closer.

The Moon attracts water on the side of Earth closest to it, making the water bulge toward it. Water also bulges on the opposite side of Earth, even though the Moon pulls less strongly on it. Coastlines in the area of the bulges have high tide at this time.

Although the Sun's gravity pulls on Earth less than half as strongly as the Moon's gravity, it, too, helps create tides.

Earth also experiences tides in its crust. The Moon's gravity can lift Earth's crust up to 5 centimeters (2 inches). Earth pulls on the Moon too and makes its surface bulge. The same is true for the other planets and moons in the solar system.

Lots of tidal activity can make a moon heat up. Materials beneath a moon's surface get hot when they are rubbed together—just as your hands warm up when you rub them together. Jupiter, for example, pulls on its moon Io so strongly that it makes Io's surface rise and fall as much as 66 meters (200 feet) or more. As a result, Io is the most volcanic body in the solar system. *SEE ALSO EARTH; IO; MOON.*

When the Sun, Moon, and Earth line up, the Sun's and Moon's gravity together produce very high tides called spring tides. When the Sun, Moon, and Earth form a letter L with Earth as the corner, the tides are lower than normal. These are called neap tides.

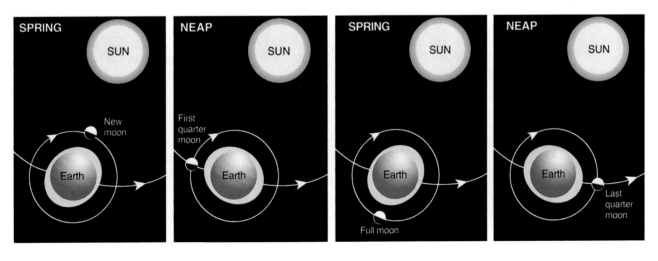

Titan

Titan is Saturn's biggest moon. It is larger than Mercury but smaller than Mars. It is named after the Titans, huge, powerful gods in ancient Greek myths. Until 1980, Titan was thought to be the largest moon in the solar system. But just as the Greek Titans were defeated by a new group of gods, so was Titan defeated by modern technology. *Voyager 1* measured Titan while flying past it in 1980. This new, more accurate measurement showed that Titan was smaller than Ganymede, Jupiter's largest moon.

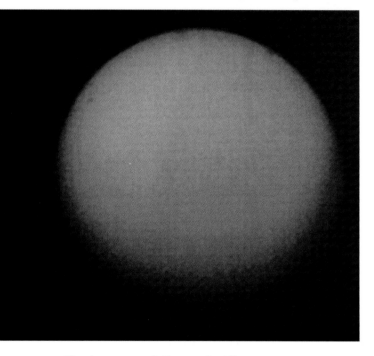

The largest of Saturn's 18 moons, Titan is smaller than Jupiter's moon Ganymede but bigger than the planets Mercury and Pluto. Titan's diameter is nearly half the size of Earth's diameter.

Titan's atmosphere hid its true size from Earthbound observers. Titan is the only moon known to have a thick atmosphere. It is an orange haze that is four times thicker than Earth's atmosphere. *Voyager 1*'s cameras could not see past this curtain of smog, but the spacecraft's other instruments easily probed the atmosphere and found it was made up mainly of nitrogen, just like Earth's atmosphere, and contained methane and other chemicals as well. *Voyager 1* also sent out radio signals as it passed behind Titan.

Scientists figured out Titan's size by studying how long the radio signals were "blacked out" by Titan.

New technology continues to peel back the layers of mystery surrounding Titan. In October 1994, the Hubble Space Telescope used a special camera to take pictures of Titan. This camera picked up wavelengths near the infrared, or heat, portion of the spectrum. The pictures showed bright and dark areas on the moon. One bright area is as big as Australia.

Scientists don't know what these areas are, but they speculate that oceans of liquid ethane and methane could cover large portions of Titan. Methane may fall from Titan's frigid atmosphere as rain and snow, covering the surface with a thick, orange material that scientists call "organic goo." An "organic" chemical compound is one that contains carbon—a basic building block of life.

Scientists are not expecting to find life on Titan. But they think that Titan's "organic goo" may hold clues to what life on the early Earth was like. In 2004, a space probe called *Huygens* will be dropped into Titan's atmosphere to find out more about this cold, distant world. It will study the atmosphere, clouds, weather, and surface. In finding out more about Titan, it may help us better understand Earth's history. SEE ALSO MOONS OF THE PLANETS; SATURN.

Tombaugh, Clyde

Clyde Tombaugh (1906–1997) was a young, amateur astronomer who discovered the planet Pluto in 1930. Tombaugh was 12 years old and a farm boy in Illinois when he first used his uncle's small telescope to look at the Moon. Afterwards, Tombaugh became fascinated with studying space. A few years later, he built his own bigger telescope. Tombaugh dreamed of being an astronomer and read every astronomy book he could find.

When a hailstorm wiped out the farm's crop in 1928, it also wrecked Tombaugh's plans to go to college. So he quickly put another plan into action. He drew pictures of Mars and Jupiter as he observed them through his homemade telescope and sent his drawings to astronomers at the Lowell Observatory

The discoverer of Pluto, astronomer Clyde Tombaugh began observing the sky as a high school student through a home-built reflecting telescope.

in Arizona. Impressed with his work, they offered him a job even though he did not have a college degree. One of his main tasks was to search for Planet X—a planet that some scientists thought existed beyond Neptune because something was causing odd wobbles in Uranus's and Neptune's orbits.

Such a search sounds exciting. It was, but Tombaugh had to be very careful and patient. To find moving objects in space, he had to take many pictures of the sky through a telescope every night. Each picture showed just a small part of the sky, dotted with thousands of stars. Tombaugh would then compare the pictures. He had to study every bit of each photo. He searched for ten months and found nothing but comets and asteroids.

Finally, on February 18, 1930, Tombaugh spotted a point of light in a picture taken on January 23, 1930. In another photo, taken on January 29, 1930, the point was in a different place. He compared it to a third photo, taken on January 21, 1930. He figured out where the point should be in the picture if it were a planet—and there it was. At age 24, Tombaugh had discovered a new planet, which was later named Pluto.

Pluto turned out to be too small to be the cause of the bigger planets' wobbling. Some scientists are still searching for another, bigger Planet X. Tombaugh won a college scholarship and became the astronomer he had always dreamed of being. *SEE ALSO PLANETS OF THE SOLAR SYSTEM; PLUTO.*

Triton

Triton is the largest of Neptune's eight moons. It is rocky, ice-covered, and almost the size of Earth's Moon. Triton's surface has flat plains and steep cliffs. It also has a strange area called "cantaloupe" land. This area is crisscrossed with icy valleys and ridges. A cap of nitrogen frost and methane ice covers Triton's southern pole. Triton also has geysers that spout tall, dark plumes. Scientists think the geysers spout when pockets of liquid nitrogen or nitrogen gas trapped beneath Triton's frozen surface heat up and explode.

Triton has a thin atmosphere of nitrogen and methane. Scientists have discovered that this atmosphere has become slightly thicker since *Voyager 2's* visit in 1989, making Triton's surface about five percent warmer.

Triton orbits Neptune in a clockwise direction. Neptune, however, spins counterclockwise. This makes Triton the only large moon in the solar system that orbits in the opposite direction of its planet's spin. Triton's odd orbital behavior may be a clue to its past. It may have been a planet like Pluto but became trapped by Neptune's gravity. Scientists think Triton and Pluto may be very similar. By studying Triton, we may also be learning about Pluto. *SEE ALSO MOONS OF THE PLANETS; NEPTUNE.*

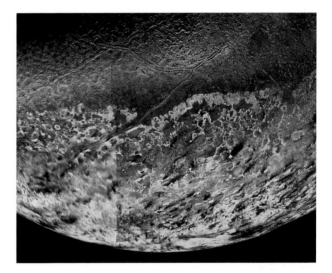

Triton's south polar cap has black smudges where geysers of liquid nitrogen may have ejected dark materials onto the surface.

Universe

The word *universe* comes from the Latin word for "whole world." Another word for universe is *cosmos*. The universe includes everything that exists— all the galaxies and all the huge stretches of space in between them. We do not know where it ends—or if it does.

What we do know is that our solar system is a tiny speck in the universe. Our Sun is one of over 100 billion stars in the Milky Way galaxy, which is just one of over 50 billion galaxies in the universe.

The galaxies are separated by vast regions of space. But they are not spread helter skelter without any pattern. Scientists describe the universe as "lumpy." Galaxies are gathered in clusters. These clusters form superclusters. Many clusters seem to cling to the edges of superclusters. Galaxies wrap around empty areas of space like a series of fences.

Nobody knows just how the universe began, but most scientists accept a theory called the Big Bang. According to the Big Bang idea, all the material of the universe was once packed into a point called a singularity. This point was not in one spot—it was everywhere, all at once. About 13 to 15 billion years ago the point exploded. The early universe expanded in all directions, and space, time, and gravity began. The universe became a hot, dark sea of energy and matter. Within this sea were areas that were a little less crowded or a little more crowded.

Over time, the new universe cooled down. Gravity pulled together material in the areas that

Two maps of the entire sky *show slight variations in the cosmic background radiation as different computer-generated colors (above left) and as thousands of X ray sources (above right), many of which may be black holes at the centers of galaxies.*

were slightly more crowded. About half a billion years after the Big Bang, gases formed clumps that were big enough and hot enough to become stars. The stars and other matter attracted each other with gravity, too, and formed the first galaxies.

The Big Bang theory is based on clues gathered in studying the universe. Some of those clues have been revealed by telescopes.

A telescope helps us see objects that are very dim and far away. It also is a peephole back in time, because many objects in the sky are so far away that their light takes a long time to reach us. For example, light from the Sun takes about 8 minutes to reach Earth. So we see the Sun the way it looked 8 minutes ago. The star Proxima Centauri is much farther from Earth. It lies about 40 trillion kilometers (25 trillion miles) away. This distance is so vast that Proxima Centauri's light takes 4.2 years to reach our eyes. So we say that this star is about 4.2 light-years away. (A light-year is the distance light travels in a year.)

With large telescopes we can see very far into the past. The Hubble Space Telescope, for example, has taken pictures of some of the universe's earliest galaxies, which may be over 12 billion years old.

Telescopes have also helped scientists discover how galaxies are moving in relation to one another. By using instruments called spectrographs to analyze the light captured by telescopes from distant galaxies, scientists noticed that these galaxies appear redder than they really are. Their light is shifted toward the red end of the spectrum—a clear sign that these objects are traveling away from us. In short, galaxies are still rushing away from one another because of the Big Bang.

Other Big Bang clues involve radio waves and microwave radiation. In 1965, scientists studying radio waves in space noticed a lot of background radio noise. Their receivers picked up a hiss coming from all directions. This radiation is left over from the Big Bang. More recently, in 1994, scientists detected ripples in this radiation, using a microwave satellite called COBE, short for Cosmic Background Explorer. These ripples could explain why the universe is lumpy. But many mysteries remain. For example, will the universe expand forever or will it someday shrink? The answer depends on dark matter.

Dark matter cannot be seen. Yet it may form about 90 percent of the material in the universe. Scientists think dark matter exists because of the way they see stars moving within galaxies. Gravity is

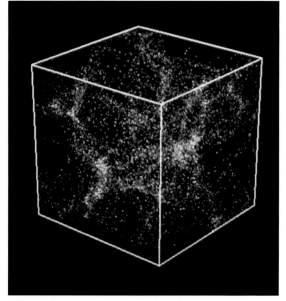

A model of a portion of the universe showing 10,000 galaxies in a cube with sides about 261 million light years long. The galaxies do not fill the space evenly but are clustered in long strings, sheets, and clumps, leaving immense spaces almost completely empty.

pulling on them, but that gravity is not coming from the other stars and objects near them. It must be coming from something invisible to us—dark matter.

The mysterious dark matter may include things incredibly huge and incredibly small. The huge items are called MACHOs. This stands for Massive Compact Halo Objects. MACHOs include black holes, asteroids, burned-out stars, and brown dwarfs. Brown dwarfs are warm objects bigger than Jupiter that do not shine. The small items are called WIMPs, or Weakly Interacting Massive Particles. Smaller than tiny atoms, they do not react with ordinary matter and don't cause anything to happen when they hit atoms. Nobody has yet found a WIMP.

But scientists are studying one kind of tiny particle known as hot dark matter, which may be made up of tiny particles called neutrinos. Smaller than atoms, billions of neutrinos are given off by the Sun and other stars.

Scientists study neutrinos deep underground in labs equipped with tanks filled with very pure water. The neutrinos make tiny flashes of light when they hit other particles. In 1998, scientists discovered that neutrinos may have mass. If neutrinos do have mass, they have gravity, too—and they might form the missing mass of the universe.

If there is enough dark matter, the universe may eventually stop expanding, collapse, and become a small, dense point again—after which it might once again expand outward in a new Big Bang. Or perhaps the universe will just keep on expanding forever. SEE ALSO BLACK HOLE; GALAXY; HUBBLE, EDWIN; MILKY WAY GALAXY.

Uranus and its moon Miranda were photographed by Voyager 2 in 1986. Researchers combined photographs to create this imaginary view of the blue-green planet encircled by rings and its rocky moon as it might appear from a passing spaceship.

Uranus

On March 13, 1781, astronomer Sir William Herschel made a discovery that changed everyone's ideas about the size of the solar system. Herschel was looking though a telescope from his garden in England, peering at the constellation Gemini. Among the stars, he spied a very small blue-green circle no one had noticed before. That circle was Uranus, which is twice as far away from the Sun as Saturn. Herschel's discovery had doubled the size of the solar system.

Uranus is a world tilted on its side. Its axis (the imaginary line from the top of a planet to the bottom around which the planet rotates) tips nearly 98 degrees from a straight-up-and-down position. (Earth's axis tips only about 23 degrees from a vertical position.) While most of the other planets spin like tops, Uranus spins sideways like a wheel. This means the Sun shines directly on Uranus's north and south poles. One pole spends 42 years bathed in sunlight as Uranus makes its 84-year journey around the Sun. Then it plunges into darkness for the next 42 years.

Uranus's magnetic axis (an imaginary line through a planet with one end acting as magnetic north and the other as magnetic south) is also tilted oddly, and it lies almost 7,700 kilometers (4,800 miles) away from the middle of the planet. As a result, Uranus's magnetic and geographic poles are far apart from one another. On Earth, the two types of poles are much closer together.

Why is Uranus so oddly tilted? Scientists think it may have crashed into an object as big as Earth long ago. The force of such a crash would have made the planet tip over.

Like its distant neighbors Jupiter, Saturn, and Neptune, Uranus is a giant planet made up mostly of gases. Its atmosphere contains much helium and hydrogen. Clouds of methane float on top of the atmosphere. Methane is a gas made of carbon and hydrogen. If you have ever smelled swamp gas, then you have gotten a whiff of methane! These clouds give Uranus its blue-green color. Scientists think that a hot, thick ocean of water, ammonia, and methane sloshes beneath the atmosphere. The planet's interior may hold liquid hydrogen, with a core of slushy rock and ice deep within.

A ring system orbits Uranus, but it cannot be seen through an ordinary telescope like Saturn's ring system can. Scientists first discovered the rings in 1977 when they watched Uranus pass in front of a star. The star flickered as the planet went by because the rings blocked the star's light. When the spacecraft *Voyager 2* flew by Uranus in 1986, sci-

URANUS Fast Facts

Mass: 14.5 x Earth
Volume: 63 x Earth
Diameter at equator: 51,118 kilometers (31,763 miles). Third largest planet
Distance from Sun: 2,871 billion kilometers (1,784 billion miles). Seventh planet from Sun
Moons: 18
Average temperature: -215°C (-355°F)
Time to rotate on axis at equator: 17 hours, 14 minutes
Time to orbit Sun: 84 years
Rings: 11
Atmosphere: Hydrogen, helium

DID YOU KNOW?
Uranus has bands of clouds like the other gas giant planets, but they are only visible in infrared photographs such as this one taken by the Hubble Space Telescope.

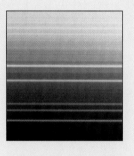

entists had a closer look at the rings. There are 11 of them, and they are made of a pitch-black material too dark to be seen from Earth. Most of the rings contain chunks that are about one meter (nearly one yard) in size. *Voyager 2* also revealed 10 new moons in addition to the five previously known. Since then, three more have been discovered, bringing the total of known Uranian moons to 18.

Voyager 2 flew within 107,100 kilometers (66,550 miles) of Uranus. It did not find much activity on its cloudy blue surface, but since 1986 some stormy weather has been observed.

Voyager 2 then sailed on past Uranus's moons, sending back spectacular images of their surfaces. For the first time we viewed Umbriel, pocked with craters and wearing a bright halo on its top, and Miranda, a craggy, cratered moon that appears to have been smashed to bits and then put back together again. Ariel, Titania, and Oberon are other large Uranian moons. SEE ALSO GAS GIANT PLANETS; MIRANDA; MOONS OF THE PLANETS.

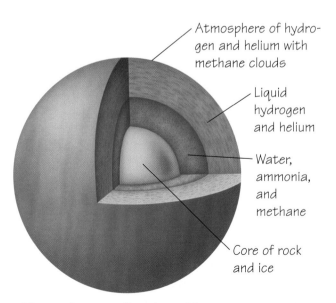

Atmosphere of hydrogen and helium with methane clouds

Liquid hydrogen and helium

Water, ammonia, and methane

Core of rock and ice

Uranus's core of rock and ice is surrounded by liquid water, ammonia, and methane. Its atmosphere is mostly hydrogen and helium. The diameter of Uranus is four times larger than Earth's.

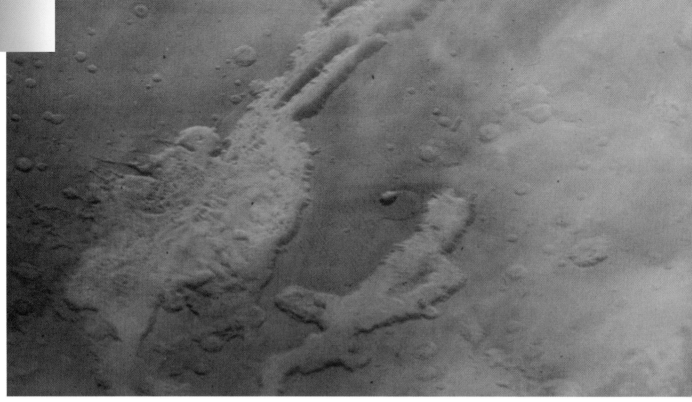

Valley of the Mariners

The Valley of the Mariners is a very long system of canyons on Mars. It is often called by its name in Latin, Valles Marineris. It stretches for 4,000 kilometers (2,500 miles) and wraps about one-fifth of the way around Mars. It plunges as deep as 8 kilometers (5 miles) below Mars's surface. That is more than three times as deep as Earth's Grand Canyon.

In satellite photographs, Valles Marineris looks like a giant, dark scar. It most likely formed when the surface of Mars was torn by strong forces. The surface ripped, just as a piece of cloth tears when pulled in a tug-of-war.

The cause of this tear may be a bulging area called the Tharsis Rise. The Tharsis Rise is a hump of land 8,000 kilometers (5,000 miles) long and 10 kilometers (6 miles) high with many volcanoes on it. Lava that erupted from these volcanoes probably helped build up the hump. The growth of the Tharsis Rise may have split Mars's surface and created Valles Marineris.

Valles Marineris is named in honor of *Mariner 9*, the first spacecraft to orbit Mars in 1971. It sent back many pictures, showing us almost all of the Martian surface. Among these images was the first picture of Valles Marineris. *SEE ALSO MARS; WATER.*

The Valley of the Mariners (also called Valles Marineris) is a giant canyon system along the Martian equator. Some channels running north from the canyon may once have contained flowing water.

Van Allen Belts

The Van Allen belts are a pair of invisible, doughnut-shaped rings around Earth. Both the inner and the outer belts are full of electrically charged particles, such as electrons and protons.

When cosmic rays and the solar wind approach Earth, they can get caught by these belts. Trapped electrons and protons are forced to travel back and forth between Earth's magnetic poles. (The magnetic poles are near but not at the same places as Earth's geographic north and south poles.)

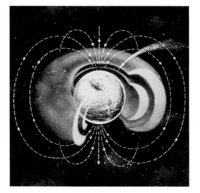

The Van Allen radiation belts circle Earth in two regions. One begins about 7,600 kilometers (4,500 miles) up; the other, about 19,000 kilometers (11,500 miles) up.

The Van Allen belts are named after the American physicist James Van Allen. In 1957, Van Allen designed an instrument to detect radiation levels around Earth. It was put on *Explorer 1*, the first U.S. satellite, which was launched on January 31, 1958. Van Allen's device detected bands of high-energy charged particles far above Earth.

The Van Allen belts are also called radiation belts. Jupiter and Saturn have radiation belts, too. Radiation belts can harm spacecraft traveling through them by damaging electrical systems, and they can make humans ill. *See also Magnetic Fields.*

Venera Series

The Venera program was a series of 16 space probes sent to Venus by the Soviet Union from 1961 to 1983. *Venera* is Russian for "Venus." After several early failures, the program became successful and scored many space history firsts.

Venus, a very bright planet as seen from Earth, is wrapped in thick clouds containing sulfuric acid. These clouds hide its surface where temperatures reach over 480°C (900°F) and the atmosphere presses down with a force 90 times stronger than Earth's. The atmosphere, which is 96 percent carbon dioxide, is poisonous to Earth-based life forms.

Venus's harsh environment is also harmful to spacecraft. It destroyed some of the Venera space probes, but the Soviets learned from these disasters and redesigned their spacecraft so they could survive.

Venera 1, launched on February 12, 1961, was the first spacecraft sent on a mission to another planet. It lost contact with Earth in just two weeks. *Venera 2* and *Venera 3* reached Venus only to break off contact before entering the planet's atmosphere.

Venera 4 had better luck. It reached Venus and released a capsule, which sent back information about air temperature, pressure, and chemical makeup as it dropped. After an hour and a half, however, it was crushed by Venus's atmospheric pressure before it could land. Engineers used this information to build a stronger and faster probe.

Venera 5 and *6* both crashed on Venus. *Venera*

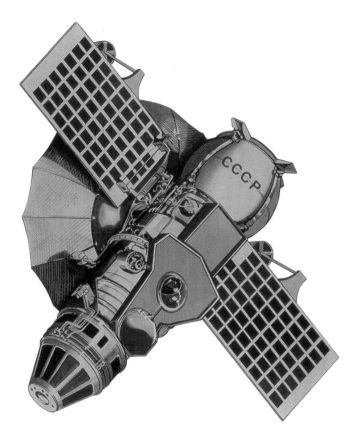

The Venera 7 spacecraft, launched in 1970, was the first to land on another planet. It was also the first spacecraft to transmit signals to Earth from another planet.

7, however, became not only the first spacecraft to land on another planet's surface but also the first spacecraft to send back signals from the surface of another planet. *Venera 7* dropped through Venus's atmosphere on December 12, 1970, and sent back information for 23 minutes.

The rest of the Venera series racked up successes, too. *Venera 8* landed on Venus in July 1972 and studied the soil. It showed that daylight on Venus was like Earth's on a cloudy, rainy day. *Venera 9* and *10* sent back the first photos, in black and white, of Venus in 1975. *Venera 11* and *12* studied Venus's dirt and atmosphere. *Venera 13* and *14* took the first color pictures of Venus in 1982.

In October 1983, *Venera 15* and *16* made radar maps of Venus's surface. These were the best maps until the United States's *Magellan* visited Venus in 1990. *See also Magellan Mission; Mariner Series; Venus.*

Normally hidden by clouds, a volcano on Venus, called Maat Mons, is revealed in this computer-generated image. It was created from radar signals sent back by the spacecraft Magellan. Lava flows (yellow areas) cover the mountain's slopes and stretch out across the plains around it.

Venus

The surface of Venus hides from Earth's telescopes beneath a blanket of clouds. These clouds are not fluffy puffs of water vapor as they are on Earth. They contain sulfuric acid, which smells like rotten eggs and can burn skin and char wood. Sulfuric acid rain falls in Venus's clouds, but the drops turn to vapor before they ever hit the ground.

Below these smelly, poisonous clouds lies Venus's intensely hot atmosphere. Temperatures on Venus shoot up to 480°C (900°F)—hot enough to melt lead. Venus is the hottest planet in the solar system, even though it is twice as far from the Sun as Mercury. About 96 percent of the atmosphere consists of carbon dioxide. Carbon dioxide lets sun-

light shine through but blocks heat from escaping. On Venus, the heat made by sunlight baking the surface is trapped by the atmosphere like hot air in a car on a summer day. This process is called the greenhouse effect.

If you were to land on Venus and somehow survive its scorching temperatures, you would still find your visit more than a little unpleasant. The atmosphere is so thick that you would not be able to see more than 100 meters (300 feet) in front of you. The pressure of the atmosphere—90 times greater than Earth's pressure—would crush you unless you were properly protected by special gear or equipment. Such pressure is as great as the pressure 1,000 meters (3,000 feet) deep in the ocean, beneath the weight of many tons of water.

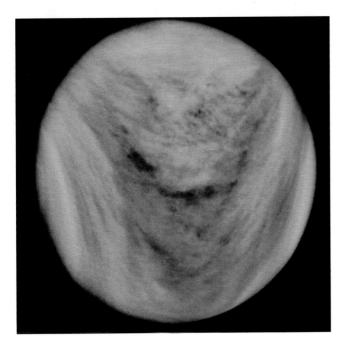

An ultraviolet photograph of Venus taken by the Galileo spacecraft reveals cloud details that are invisible in normal light. Clouds of sulfuric acid droplets in the upper atmosphere of Venus swirl around the planet every four or five Earth days.

VENUS Fast Facts

Mass: 0.8 x Earth
Volume: 0.9 x Earth
Diameter at equator: 12,104 kilometers (7,521 miles). Sixth largest planet
Distance from Sun: 108 million kilometers (67 million miles). Second planet from Sun
Moons: 0
Average temperature: 480°C (900°F)
Time to rotate on axis: 243 days
Time to orbit Sun: 225 days
Rings: No
Atmosphere: Carbon dioxide

DID YOU KNOW? Venus is the brightest and hottest planet in the solar system.

In the past, Earth and Venus were thought of as "twin sister planets." Venus is indeed almost as big as Earth and comes closer to Earth than any other planet, but the two planets are vastly different.

Venus does not even spin in the same direction as Earth. It rotates clockwise. As a result, on Venus the Sun rises in the west and sets in the east. But Venus spins so slowly, you would hardly notice the Sun moving in the sky. It takes 243 Earth days to spin once on its axis, while it takes just 225 Earth days to orbit the Sun. Thus, Venus's *day* is 18 Earth days longer than its *year.* Although Venus is closer to the Sun than Earth is, a day on Venus would be only as bright as a rainy day on Earth. Venus's clouds dim the light that reaches the planet's surface.

From Earth, though, Venus is so bright it can be seen without a telescope at dawn and dusk. Often called the morning or evening star, Venus is the brightest object in the sky after the Sun and Moon. Venus looks bright to us because so much sunlight bounces off the planet's thick clouds.

Venus's thick clouds and hostile environment posed challenges to exploration but did not prevent it. The Soviet Union sent probes to Venus in the 1960s, 1970s, and 1980s. Some sent back data and pictures. Others orbited Venus and sent radio signals that guided computers in creating the first radar maps of Venus's surface. The United States also sent probes to Venus. *Mariner 2* rocketed into space in 1962, becoming the first spacecraft to fly by Venus. *Magellan,* launched in 1989, orbited Venus more than 15,000 times in four years and made detailed radar maps.

These maps show that Venus has highlands and lowlands like Earth's plains and ocean basins. It has volcanoes with broad domes, called shield volcanoes, like those in Hawaii. Giant volcanic "spiders," called arachnoids, sprawl on Venus, too. They are volcanic craters surrounded by long, winding cracks.

Fewer than 1,000 impact craters (craters dug out when big objects crashed into the planet) mark Venus. Scientists think a lava flow may have repaved half of Venus 500 million years ago—just yesterday on a planet that is 4.6 billion years old—and that Venus's volcanoes still erupt. Venus is named for the Roman goddess of love. *SEE ALSO GREENHOUSE EFFECT; MAGELLAN MISSION; MARINER SERIES; PLANETARY CORES; PLANETS OF THE SOLAR SYSTEM; VENERA SERIES.*

Viking Program

In 1976, two Viking space probes called landers touched down on Mars. Both were dropped from orbiters which circled Mars, received information from the landers, and relayed it to Earth. *Viking 1* landed on July 20, becoming the first probe to arrive safely on Mars. *Viking 2* landed about 7,400 kilometers (4,600 miles) away on August 7.

Both landers sent images to Earth showing red soil and rocks beneath a reddish sky but no living things. Experiments failed to find life, too. Robot arms scooped up soil samples and delivered them to special compartments for testing. Some tests came back positive for gases associated with life, but one of the most important tests did not find any chemicals in the soil suggesting that life was present.

The Viking landers discovered that Martian soil is dry and full of iron; its atmosphere is mostly carbon dioxide; and levels of ultraviolet rays are so high they would be deadly to most Earth life forms.

Viking 2 kept working until 1980. *Viking 1* worked until 1982—long after it was expected to run out of power. SEE ALSO LIFE; MARINER SERIES; MARS.

A Viking 2 lander image shows a portion of the spacecraft with an American flag. In the background beneath a pink sky lies the reddish Martian surface strewn with hundreds of dark boulders.

Volcanoes

A volcano is a hole or crack in a planet's crust through which magma (hot, melted rock) escapes from inside the planet. Magma is called lava when it is on a planet's surface. Many volcanoes are mountains made from lava that hardened and built up around such holes over millions of years.

Sometimes, heat and pressure inside Earth force melted rock through weak parts of Earth's crust. The crust is broken into pieces that fit together like a jigsaw puzzle. Often, the weakest areas are where two pieces, called plates, of Earth's crust meet.

When gases inside magma expand, they force magma out of Earth's crust. Magma can ooze out onto Earth's surface through cracks in the sea floor. Magma can also erupt from volcanoes. The magma builds and shapes the volcano over time.

Earth boasts about 600 active volcanoes. Some are parts of mountain chains on the continents. Others rise from the ocean floor. Volcanoes come in different shapes. Shield volcanoes are large domes built by layers of lava. Kilauea, an active Hawaiian volcano, is a shield volcano. Stratovolcanoes are shaped like cones with a crater scooped out of the top. They contain layers of lava and ash. Mount Fuji in Japan and Mount Rainier in Washington State are stratovolcanoes.

Other planets and even moons in our solar system have volcanoes. In fact, the biggest shield volcano in the solar system is on Mars. It is called Olympus Mons and stands 24 kilometers (15 miles) tall. (Mt. Everest, the highest point on Earth, is less than 6 miles high.) Scientists have also found flat areas on Mars that seem to have been created by lava flows carrying rafts of solid lava. Some of these flows may have occurred as recently as 200 million years ago.

Venus's young surface has been widely repaved by lava. It

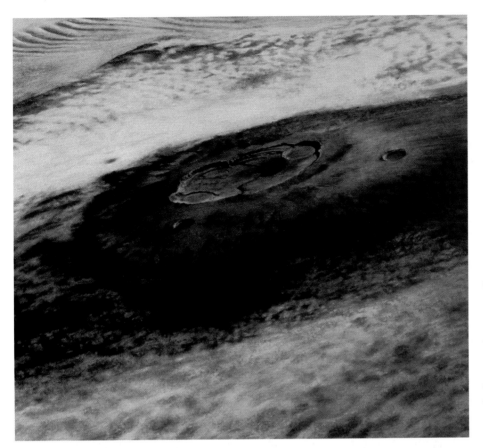

The giant volcano Olympus Mons looms 8 kilometers (5 miles) above the clouds in this photo of Mars taken by a Viking orbiter. The largest volcano in the solar system, it extends over an area larger than New England.

has shield volcanoes as well as types of volcanoes that don't exist on Earth. One of these odd volcanoes is called an arachnoid, which means spider. An arachnoid is a volcanic crater circled by rings and long cracks. These features make it look like a long-legged spider sitting in a giant web. Venus also has pancake domes—wide, flat volcanoes that may have formed when lava flowed out evenly in all directions.

The hot spot of the solar system, however, is not a planet but a moon. That moon is Io, which orbits Jupiter. It is the most volcanically active object in the solar system. Io's volcanoes are fueled by heat generated inside Io as it is pulled back and forth by Jupiter and two other moons, Europa and Ganymede. This tug-of-war squeezes and expands Io, causing rubbing, or friction, that heats up and melts rock into magma inside it. Eventually, the magma erupts.

In 1979, *Voyager 1* took photos of Io. These showed plumes of volcanic material rising over 500 kilometers (310 miles) above a volcano called Pele that is as wide as the state of Alaska. *Voyager 1* also revealed that Io's colorful surface is streaked with

orange, brown, and yellow—evidence of sulfur in Io's surface. Scientists think Io's lava is made of rocks containing sulfur. Sulfur dioxide gas from volcanoes freezes to form sulfur dioxide frost.

Io's active volcanoes have wiped out all traces of its ancient past. It has no impact craters made by asteroids or meteorites. Instead, Io's craters are all volcanic ones, called caldera. *SEE ALSO IO; MARS; MOON; VENUS.*

Von Braun, Wernher

Wernher von Braun (1912–1977) was an engineer who developed rockets for the United States's space program. During World War II, he was the director of a rocket research center that developed military missiles for Germany.

After the war von Braun began working in the United States on the American rocket program. His team of engineers developed the Redstone rocket, which launched some of the United States's Mercury program spacecraft, and also produced the rocket that launched the first U.S. satellite into orbit in 1958. In the 1960s, von Braun headed up the development of the Saturn V rockets, which launched the Apollo spacecraft into space on their journeys to the Moon. *SEE ALSO APOLLO PROGRAM.*

Voyager Mission

Two Voyager spacecraft stunned the world with new discoveries about the gas giant planets—Jupiter, Saturn, Uranus, and Neptune.

Voyager 2 was launched on August 20, 1977. Sixteen days later, *Voyager 1* was launched on a shorter, faster path to Jupiter. It arrived first, in March 1979, and sent back data about Jupiter's magnetic field, its atmosphere, its moon Io, and a thin ring it discovered circling the planet.

Then *Voyager 1* traveled to Saturn, reaching it in November 1980. Images showed that the big rings around the planet were made up of thousands of smaller rings. *Voyager 1* also discovered new moons orbiting Saturn, swooped close to the moon Titan, and then headed off to the edge of the solar system.

Voyager 2 took a longer journey, visiting not only Jupiter and Saturn but also Uranus and Neptune because Earth and the gas giant planets happened to be lined up in a curve at the time.

At Jupiter, *Voyager 2* focused on Io and the newly discovered ring. Then it headed for Saturn

Passing by Jupiter in 1979, *Voyager 2 (below, right) sent back pictures of the Great Red Spot (below) showing that it is a huge storm. Later, Voyager 2 reached Neptune and revealed that its temporary dark spot was a hole in the atmosphere.*

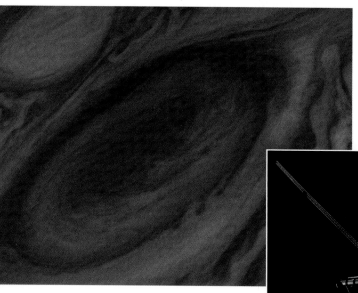

and on to Uranus, where it studied rings and discovered 10 moons. Finally, *Voyager 2* traveled to Neptune where it spotted dim rings and storms in the atmosphere. It also found six new moons before heading off into outer space.

Both *Voyager 1* and *2* are still in touch with scientists. The Voyager project is now called the Voyager Interstellar Mission. Its main goal is to travel beyond Pluto's orbit to a place where the Sun's magnetic field ends and the solar wind dies. By the year 2020, the Voyagers will likely run out of power.

Each ship carries messages for any intelligent beings that might find them! Gold-plated phonograph records are attached to each ship, containing songs of birds and humpback whales, music, words spoken in 56 languages, and photos of life on Earth. *SEE ALSO EXPLORATION OF THE SOLAR SYSTEM.*

Water

Water covers about three-quarters of Earth's surface. No other planet in the solar system has oceans, rivers, and lakes like Earth's.

Water is vital to life on Earth. Many millions of years ago, life developed in the oceans. Living things rely on water for the chemical reactions that support life. About 75 percent of your body consists of water. Your blood is 80 percent water. Water shapes rocks, makes weather, and keeps Earth's temperature from swinging wildly. Water is everywhere—in the air as a gas and in the ground and the oceans as liquid and ice.

Water also exists on other planets and on moons. Mars has plains and channels that were most likely created by floods and rivers of water. Where did that water go? Much of it may have drifted off into space as water vapor. The rest is frozen in Mars's soil and in its polar caps along with carbon dioxide frost. Venus has no oceans today, but water does form in its clouds. Jupiter's atmosphere contains some water vapor. Saturn's atmosphere also contains water vapor, and its rings include chunks of ice. Uranus and Neptune may have oceans of water, methane, and ammonia beneath their icy clouds.

The gas giant planets have many ice-covered moons. Two of Jupiter's moons, Europa and Callisto, may even have salty oceans beneath their icy surfaces. Our own Moon may have water, too. In 1998, the spacecraft *Lunar Prospector* detected signs of water at the Moon's north and south poles.

In your reading you may encounter the term *water ice*. There are other kinds of ice besides water ice. Pluto has ice made of methane. Methane ice floats high in Neptune's atmosphere. Jupiter has ammonia ice in its upper atmosphere. You may have seen frozen carbon dioxide, called dry ice, here on Earth. *SEE ALSO CALLISTO; COMETS; EARTH; EUROPA; MARS.*

X rays

X rays are part of the electromagnetic spectrum. This spectrum also includes radio waves, microwaves, and light rays. All are forms of radiation, or energy. Light rays are the only ones we can see. The rest are invisible to our eyes.

On Earth, we often use X rays to see inside objects and living things. How X rays travel through something depends on the material. Bones block X rays and show up white on film.

In space, X rays are produced by many objects, such as exploding stars and young galaxies called quasars. Black holes in the process of swallowing up stars are revealed by X rays. Magnetic fields that capture electrically charged particles also give off X rays. Earth's atmosphere blocks these X rays, so scientists put X-ray telescopes into orbit above the atmosphere. The first satellite to use X rays for astronomy, called *Uhuru*, was sent aloft in 1970. The Chandra X-Ray Observatory (named after the late Indian-American Nobel Prize winner S. Chandrasekhar) was launched by a space shuttle in 1999. It is mapping the entire sky and studying black holes, novas, the Sun, quasars, and galaxies. *SEE ALSO BLACK HOLE; GALAXY; SPECTRUM; TELESCOPES.*

Zap Crater

A zap crater, also known as a microcrater or zap pit, is a tiny pit that forms when a particle in space strikes a satellite or spacecraft. Zap craters can be caused by meteoroids or by space trash—garbage in space created by humans. A lot of this orbiting trash is so small that it can only be seen with a microscope, but some bits are quite large. For example, the *Apollo 13* Lunar Module, which was ejected in space in 1970, is still in orbit around Earth!

Meteoroids and bits of space trash can dot a spacecraft with zap craters. One satellite had 186 zap craters, about 176 of which were caused by flecks of paint from other satellites! A tiny paint fleck chipped the window of the shuttle *Challenger* in 1983. Such little particles can cause damage because they travel about 25,000 kilometers (17,500 miles) per hour). *SEE ALSO METEOROIDS.*

Zodiacal dust is visible in this photograph as a reddish glow in the sky directly over the place where the Sun has set.

Zodiacal Dust

Zodiacal dust is dust drifting about in the inner solar system. This dust is made up of tiny bits of comets and asteroids. It lies along part of the plane on which the inner planets travel around the Sun. Zodiacal dust can be seen in clear skies after sunset or before sunrise. The dust forms a dim, cone-shaped area of soft light spreading above the spot where the Sun rose or set. It glows because it reflects sunlight. *SEE ALSO ASTEROIDS; COMETS.*

ammonia—a chemical compound made of nitrogen and hydrogen. It is found in the atmosphere of the gas giant planets and is used on Earth in cleaning fluids.

axis—an imaginary pole that runs through the center of an object, around which the object rotates.

carbon—an element that is part of all living things. It also exists as a mineral (such as a diamond) and as part of a gas (such as carbon dioxide).

carbon dioxide—a gas made up of carbon and oxygen. On Earth, carbon dioxide is a gas that animals breathe out and plants take in. The atmospheres of Venus and Mars are mostly carbon dioxide.

core—the heavy, dense center of a planet, moon, or star.

eclipse—the lining up of space objects in such a way that one throws a shadow on the other. Eclipses of the Sun and Moon occur when Earth lines up with them in a particular way, and either Earth blocks sunlight from reaching the Moon (lunar eclipse) or the Moon blocks sunlight from reaching Earth (solar eclipse).

electromagnetic spectrum—the range of energy (electro-magnetic radiation) produced by stars, chemicals, and other natural objects. It includes radio waves, microwaves, infrared (heat) waves, visible light, ultraviolet light, X rays, and gamma rays.

equator—an imaginary line that wraps around the middle of a planet, moon, or star like a belt, lying exactly in between its north and south poles.

greenhouse effect—the warming of a planet's surface caused by heat trapped in the planet's atmosphere.

helium—an element that is a gas. It is one of the two main components of the Sun and other stars and the gas giant planets. (The other main element is hydrogen.) On Earth, helium is used to fill balloons and blimps.

hydrogen—an element that is a gas. It is one of the two main components of the Sun and other stars and the gas giant planets. (The other main element is helium.)

infrared—electromagnetic radiation that cannot be seen but can be felt as heat. It can be observed by special infrared cameras, which take pictures of faraway space objects that would otherwise be invisible, or nearly so.

light-year—the distance light travels in a year, which is about 9.5 trillion kilometers (6 trillion miles). It is used to measure huge distances between space objects.

magnetic field—the area of space around a planet or star affected by its magnetic force.

mass—the amount of material in an object. A dense object is one that contains much material in a small amount of space. An object's mass is always the same, though its weight changes depending on the strength of the gravity pulling on it.

methane—a gas made up of carbon and hydrogen. On Earth it is also called "swamp gas." Methane exists in space and on Earth. Neptune gets its blue color from methane clouds in its atmosphere.

moon—a chunk or ball of rock that orbits a planet or asteroid as a natural satellite.

nebula—a cloud of gas and dust in space.

nitrogen—an element. On Earth, nitrogen is a gas that makes up 78 percent of the atmosphere.

orbit—the path traveled by one space object around another, such as a moon around a planet or a planet around the Sun. Orbits can be very long, narrow ellipses or nearly circular, like those of the planets.

oxygen—an element. On Earth, oxygen makes up 21 percent of the atmosphere as a gas, combines with other elements to form rocks and water, and sustains life forms. It is Earth's most plentiful element.

ozone—a form of oxygen that exists as a layer high in Earth's atmosphere and blocks harmful radiation from the Sun.

payload—objects, satellites, or other equipment launched into space aboard a rocket or space shuttle.

poles—the northern and southern ends of a star, planet, or moon.

regolith—the rocky, dusty layer of dirt found on moons, asteroids, and planets such as Mars.

satellite—an object in orbit around another object. A moon is a natural satellite. A space probe orbiting an object is a man-made satellite.

space probe—an unpiloted spacecraft sent into space to explore the Moon, Sun, or other planets.

weight—a measurement of the gravitational force that is pulling on an object. An object weighs more on Earth than it does on the Moon because Earth's gravity is stronger than the Moon's gravity.

zero gravity—weightlessness. An astronaut feels weightless while orbiting Earth in a spacecraft and can float freely because both the astronaut and the craft are "falling" around Earth at the same speed. Earth's gravity, however, is pulling on them both and keeping them from flying off into space.

For More Information

Books

Close Encounters: Exploring the Universe with the Hubble Space Telescope by Elaine Scott (New York: Hyperion Books for Children, 1998)

Eyewitness Books: Space Exploration by Carole Stott (New York: Alfred A. Knopf, 1997)

Fast Forward: Space Shuttle by Mark Bergin (Danbury, Connecticut: Franklin Watts, 1999)

The History of Rockets by Ron Miller (Danbury, Connecticut: Franklin Watts, 1999)

The New York Public Library Amazing Space: A Book of Answers for Kids by Ann-Jeanette Campbell (New York: John Wiley & Sons, Inc., 1997)

The Kingfisher Young People's Book of Space by Martin Redfern (New York: Kingfisher, 1998)

Mission to Deep Space: Voyager's Journey of Discovery by William E. Burrows (New York: W.H. Freeman and Co., 1993)

On the Shuttle: Eight Days in Space by Barbara Bondar (Toronto, Ontario: Greey de Pencier Books, 1993)

One Small Square: The Night Sky by Donald M. Silver (New York: Learning Triangle Press, 1998)

Pathfinders: Space by Alan Dyer (Pleasantville, New York: Reader's Digest Children's Books, 1999)

To Space and Back by Sally Ride (New York: Beech Tree, William Morrow & Co., 1991)

Space Encyclopedia by Heather Couper and Nigel Henbest (New York: Dorling Kindersley, 1999)

Space Explained: A Beginner's Guide to the Universe by Robin Scagell (New York: Henry Holt, 1996)

Space Station Science: Life in Free Fall by Marianne J. Dyson (New York: Scholastic, 1999)

Websites

Ask an Astronaut
http://www.nss.org/askastro/
An archive of questions that have been asked of astronauts.

Explore the Solar System
http://liftoff.msfc.nasa.gov/academy/space/solarsystem/
solarsystemjava.html
See the orbits and current positions of the planets and rotate the image to get a view from different angles in the solar system.

Imagine the Universe
http://imagine.gsfc.nasa.gov/docs/homepage.html
A site aimed at space explorers 14 years of age and up.

Jet Propulsion Laboratory Homepage
http://www.jpl.nasa.gov
Find news about the JPL and up-to-the-minute information about missions such as Cassini, Galileo-Europa, and Stardust.

Kennedy Space Center Homepage
http://www.ksc.nasa.gov/ksc.html
Information about the Kennedy Space Center and space shuttle missions.

NASA Homepage
http://www.nasa.gov
Offers links to NASA missions and other information about the solar system and space exploration.

NASA's Observatorium
http://observe.ivv.nasa.gov/
Pictures and information about the solar system, plus fun and games.

Nine Planets
http://seds.lpl.arizona.edu/nineplanets/nineplanets/
nineplanets.html
In-depth information about the solar system, including history, mythology, and music as well as scientific information.

Nine Planets Just for Kids
http://www.tcsn.net/afiner
Information about the solar system for kids in the upper grades of elementary school.

The Planetary Society
http://www.planetary.org
Space information and activities for all ages.

Solar System Scale Model
http://www.exploratorium.edu/ronh/solar_system/
Build your own scale model of the solar system using calculations provided by this site.

Spacelink
http://spacelink.nasa.gov/Spacelink.Cool.Picks/
A feature on Spacelink that will take you to a variety of interesting space-related sites.

The Space Place
http://spaceplace.jpl.nasa.gov/
Things to make and do, plus Dr. Marc's Amazing Facts!

StarChild
http://starchild.gsfc.nasa.gov/docs/StarChild/
A site where young astronomers can explore the solar system, hosted by the Goddard Space Flight Center.

US SpaceCamp
http://www.spacecamp.com/
Find out about U.S. SpaceCamp and what it takes to become a SpaceCamp astronaut.

The Virtual Solar System
http://www.nationalgeographic.com/solarsystem
Tours of the solar system in 2-D and 3-D, as well as information about the Sun, planets, Moon, and other solar system features.

Windows to the Universe
http://www.windows.umich.edu/
Information about earth and space sciences, including an "ask a scientist" feature.

Index

Photo/Illustration Credits